Reading Danna Bodenheimer's *Real World Clinical Social Work: Find Your Voice and Find Your Way* is like spending a weekend in a wonderful candid conversation with many of our favorite theorists! While sharing her own perspectives and experiences, Bodenheimer invites us to reflect on topics as far-ranging as the essential components of the different modalities we can use in assessing and addressing client needs to identifying the elements that are critical to both the effectiveness of our professional practice and the sustenance of our personal lives. In language that is accessible, oftentimes metaphoric, and yet not at all simplistic, this book also introduces us to some of the clinical experiences of clients and therapists through an interweaving of their stories and theories. Just prior to presenting us with a thoughtful array of "post graduate options" for further learning and development, Bodenheimer explores the dimensions and dilemmas associated with still-controversial subjects like clients' transference and clinicians' countertransference, including feelings of love. Whether just entering the world of a master's-prepared social worker or having spent decades as an agency-based or private practitioner, an educator, or an administrator in the social services, spending time with *Real World Clinical Social Work* is a real gift to yourself and everyone you serve.

Darlyne Bailey, Ph.D, ACSW, LISW
Dean, Professor, and MSS Program Director
Graduate School of Social Work and Social Research, Bryn Mawr College

As students graduate from our MSW program, they often express a mix of excitement and anticipation about beginning social work practice. They almost always wonder, "Am I ready to do this work?" Dr. Bodenheimer's book is a wonderful bridge for new graduates as they move from the support of graduate education and agency supervision to independent practitioners. Using years of teaching and astute practice experience, she provides continued education, support, and clinical insight. While grounded solidly in practice theory, Dr. Bodenheimer guides practitioners to find their own practice wisdom and style that is so essential to the social work profession. No doubt, new social workers will find this an accessible, practical primer...and a life raft for embarking on the profession!

Anne Marcus Weiss, LSW, MSW
Director of Field Education
University of Pennsylvania
School of Social Policy & Practice

Danna Bodenheimer has written an insider's guide to clinical social work that doesn't make the reader feel like an outsider. This book is the clinical supervisor you always wanted to have: brilliant yet approachable, professional yet personal, grounded and practical, yet steeped in theory, and challenging you to dig deeper.

Jonathan B. Singer, Ph.D., LCSW
Associate Professor of Social Work
Loyola University Chicago
Founder and Host, Social Work Podcast

It is nearly impossible to begin a career as a budding clinical social worker without the accompaniment of a variably loud inner voice that says, "You have no idea what you are doing." Dr. Bodenheimer befriends the beginning clinician with this incredibly personable and accessible book and says, "Sure, you do." Dr. Bodenheimer uses herself as a vehicle for connection with the reader, and she speaks directly to that inner voice with compassion, understanding, and guidance.

Cara Segal, Ph.D.
Smith College School for Social Work, faculty
Private Practitioner, Northampton, MA

Real World Clinical Social Work

Find Your Voice and Find Your Way

Danna R. Bodenheimer

The New Social Worker® PRESS

Harrisburg, Pennsylvania

Real World Clinical Social Work
Find Your Voice and Find Your Way

Danna R. Bodenheimer

Published by:

The New Social Worker®
PRESS

Post Office Box 5390
Harrisburg, PA 17110-0390 U.S.A.
717-238-3787 (voice)
717-238-2090 (fax)
http://www.socialworker.com

The New Social Worker Press is an imprint of White Hat Communications.

Note: The names and identities of social work clients mentioned in this book have been carefully disguised in accordance with professional standards of confidentiality.

Cover images from BigStockPhoto.com © Tidarat (background) and Hellena13 (speech bubbles).

Library of Congress Cataloging-in-Publication Data

Bodenheimer, Danna R.
  Real world clinical social work : find your voice and find your way / Danna R. Bodenheimer.
     pages cm
  Includes bibliographical references and index.
  ISBN 978-1-929109-50-0 (pbk.)
  1. Medical social work. 2. Social case work. 3. Social service–Practice. I. Title.
  HV687.B63 2016
  362.1'0425–dc23
                              2015032088

Contents

Acknowledgments

My most profound acknowledgment for the writing of this book goes directly to my editor, Linda May Grobman. I have read so many acknowledgment pages of writers that I love and have read many thank-yous to editors before. I now know what they have all meant. Linda met me at a rest stop in Harrisburg more than three years ago and took a real chance on me. I think we ordered apple pie, and it was delicious. I had never been to Harrisburg and she had never taken a risk like this. We both just hung in there with each other. She has been interminably patient, meticulous, and supportive. She has taken my writing and made it more accessible and legible to the audience that she knows so expertly—social workers. My freshman high school English teacher had similar critiques of my writing to Linda. My sentences are long and my paragraphs are even longer. More than 20 years later, my writing foibles remain stubborn, but not as stubborn as Linda's patient tenderness and editorial dexterity.

I would also like to thank Lina Hartocollis for her constant confidence in my clinical and academic abilities. She has been a cheerleader since I met her. Every social worker should have someone as clearly on their side as Lina has been on mine.

I also have several colleagues that I want to thank. First, I would like to acknowledge Jonathan Singer for his constant and steady presence in my intellectual and personal life. He is a dear friend and a dear scholar. I would like to thank Susan Mankita for her careful, thoughtful, and kind feedback on this book. She added a tremendous amount to the evolution of this work, and her efforts mean a tremendous amount to me. To Rachel McKay, my dear supervisor, who inspires my intellect while pushing me clinically forward in scary and essential ways—thank you. There have been times when I have experienced tremendous clinical fear, and I have felt emboldened by the steady support of Cara Segal. I am proud to call her a friend and a colleague. The same can be said of Stacey Novack, a constant thinker, who wrote me a recommendation to social work school and called me a "therapist" long before I ever earned the title. Finally, Jennifer Bryan, a psychologist, scholar, consultant, and kindred spirit—I am aware of having her spirit with me more than I can even describe.

Lisa, my confidante, your tender listening ear and ability to place my struggles in the context of age-old stories of ancestry and tradition always serve to make me feel less alone and more alive.

I would like to thank Randi Singer. Once a neighbor, now a part of my chosen family, you are such an incredible constant and force of inspiration, modeling what friendship and unconditional love and support means. I would also like to thank my parents, Carol and Ted, for lending me a writing space on the 20th floor above New York City whenever I needed it. Their persistent and unyielding belief in me has proven to be quite the secure base from which I can explore both my mind and the world.

My wife, Kira, has always been my battery charger. No matter how empty I feel as if I am running, I can anchor myself by her calming soul and find a spark for life, for writing, for thinking, for parenting, for being a social work clinician and professor. Before meeting her, I was working in an investment bank. Nearly 15 years later, I am comfortably doing my life's work day in and day out. I truly attribute this to being so clearly seen by Kira, who has believed in me unequivocally, from minute one. I think she wondered how I would finish a book while we were co-parenting two tiny boys together. She wondered—she never doubted, though.

And to those two tiny boys, who are not so tiny, you are everything. Nate and Levi, you are sweet and wise beyond compare and have truly taught me the difference between nature and nurture (there is one—I didn't know). Your love of animals, of life, of joy, of laughter, and of knowledge makes me so much hope for the world. I only hope that one day you will be as proud of me as I am of you.

Foreword

Anyone who has been involved in social work education, whether as a teacher or learner, is likely familiar with the concept of "integrating theory with practice." This refers, of course, to the importance of having a knowledge base that guides our practice. In other words, it is code for "don't fly by the seat of your pants." Students of social work spend several years in the classroom busily learning about the history and values of the social work profession; social work ethics; theories—developmental, social, psychological, and social work-specific—that undergird and inform practice; skills—how to listen to clients, assess, build a helping relationship, set tasks and goals, document the work, end responsibly; and so on. But the reality is that social work students are often so busy taking all this wonderful content in that they don't have the time or focus to put it all together. In the end, it takes not only a good curriculum but good teachers to help students thoughtfully, carefully, and deliberately integrate what they've learned into their practice.

The qualities that make for a good social work teacher are not so different from the qualities of a good social work clinician. Good clinicians and teachers are highly knowledgeable and well-prepared. They are able to connect with their students or clients in a structured, supportive, purposeful way. They create an atmosphere that feels safe but also encourages risk-taking and venturing beyond what's comfortable. They help capture and make sense of real world experiences and deftly weave in teachable in-vivo moments. Last, but definitely not least, they use themselves as finely tuned instruments to both model and encourage the qualities and skills they are trying to develop. In the end, the best teachers and clinicians have in common a well-honed and distinctive style of teaching or practice that both grounds and frees them.

In this wonderful primer on clinical social work practice, Dr. Danna Bodenheimer's prodigious experience and talents as a social work clinician and educator are in full view. She has crafted a beautifully written, down-to-earth, and highly practical guide to help beginning social workers develop their own practice style and professional identity. I first came to know Danna when she was a student in the University of Pennsylvania's Doctorate in Clinical Social Work

(DSW) program. She was a teaching assistant in a master's-level social work class on mental health diagnostics. Later, we co-taught together, and I invited her back to my class each semester to present a guest lecture on addictions, one of her many areas of clinical expertise. I marveled at the sea of hands that remained in the air throughout much of the class when Danna taught, as students clamored to share their thoughts and ideas. Even the typically quiet students joined in, emboldened by Danna's thoughtful, accepting responses to their classmates' contributions. I remember well how humbling it was to see Danna in action and to realize that, despite my combined 30 years of practice and teaching experience, she was every bit as good a teacher as I, if not better!

Danna is truly a remarkable educator who uses herself and her experiences—professional, and when appropriate, personal—to guide her students through the complicated terrain of clinical practice. She deftly brings in examples from her own and her students' practice to make the learning come to life. She has mastered the art of formulating and asking questions in a way that engages, stimulates generative discussion, and produces the sort of "aha!" experiences in students that all good teachers strive for. It is no wonder that she became one of our most popular teachers. A recipient of the School's prestigious Excellence in Teaching Award, students lined up to get into her classes.

Danna brings the same participatory, wise, Socratic style to this book. Picking up where MSW programs leave off, she guides the reader on a wild and wonderful tour of clinical social work practice—everything the conscientious, committed, well trained social worker needs to know. She starts with the all-important basics— what exactly is clinical social work and what essential principles are at its core, and then moves to why trauma work and clinical social work are one and the same, how we can integrate psychodynamic and cognitive theories into practice, the ways in which clinical social work happens in pretty much any practice setting—from agency-based, to medical, to school, to mental health, and the importance of good supervision and how to get it. One of my favorite parts of the book is "what I wish I'd known"—practical tips and words of wisdom from real social workers as they reflect on their own professional journeys. The book includes a brave look at two of the most taboo topics in clinical social work—love (why it's okay for our clients to love us and for us to love them), and money (why it's okay to be fairly paid for what we do).

Using powerful case examples and a series of carefully crafted questions, this book challenges readers to think broadly and deeply about their own social work practice and identity. It is an invaluable companion for beginning social workers and educators alike.

Lina Hartocollis, Ph.D., LCSW
Dean of Students
Director, Doctorate in Clinical Social Work (DSW) Program
University of Pennsylvania
School of Social Policy & Practice

Preface
What Do We Have Here?

For me, personally, I have found the idea of clinical social work confusing. I have had an excellent sense of what social work is for a long time. I have even really understood the idea of clinical work well, but mostly through the lens of psychology. However, clinical social work, as an entity, has sometimes felt like an elusive notion. We all take the history of social work in graduate school, but the actual ways in which theory has informed clinical social work practice is fairly opaque. There is a way in which clinical social work can feel like a patchwork of theoretical modalities that are hand-me-downs from psychology (cognitive behavioral therapy, behavioral therapy), analytic schools of thought (object relations, ego psychology, self psychology), philosophy (narrative work, critical race theory), and current research done in psychiatry (neurobiology, addiction treatments).

It can be hard to find *our own,* or more importantly, *your own* style when your wardrobe is filled with hand-me-downs. Sure, there are clothes that are definitely ours—such as empowerment theory, strengths-based work, and systems theory. But when working with individuals, you might start to find that you need more layers—a sweatshirt, tights, maybe a spring jacket. And these items weren't necessarily chosen for you, but you need to find a way to make them fit. Practicing clinical social work well means finding your style amidst of sea of powerful echoes from other fields and then making that style all your own. It can be liberating and innovative, but it is not easy.

This book is designed to help you find your own design, your own style, and your own path toward becoming a clinical social worker. And not just a clinical social worker, but a clinical social worker who has tremendous authorship over your own career, the ability to effect micro and macro level change, and a social worker who can make enough money to live and breathe with some air to spare.

This book is written for new graduates and more senior practitioners alike. If you just graduated, this book is certainly perfect for you. If you are thinking about entering a more clinical realm within our field, this book is certainly perfect for you, as well. It is a map around the world of clinical social work that will particularly work to support you when navigating the more choppy terrain within our field. To help you with that navigation, this book includes a tremendous amount of insight by clinical social workers who have "been there." Specifically, data are provided from a survey that was performed upon 100 social workers. All respondents have at least five years post-graduate experience, work in a variety of settings, and identify as somehow "clinical." I posted the survey on several websites frequented by social workers, and they responded with information about their level of satisfaction in the field, their salaries, the amount of debt they hold, and other pieces of information that will illuminate muddy waters.

I started to realize, through my teaching and practice, that I was in a unique position to synthesize a tremendous amount of information about the field of clinical social work. I have had access to many students, syllabi from different MSW programs, new graduates, and even clients who are in the field. I have woven together what I have found and learned, and put it all here, in one space. This book is for anyone who is looking to have a resource that refines the search for the essential information that one needs when starting in this incredibly diverse, often confusing, and even more often thrilling field of work.

I started writing this book about three years ago. My dog's hair wasn't gray, but it is now. Fortunately, mine isn't. That is because writing this book hasn't been particularly taxing. It has evolved somewhat organically out of years of conversation with fellow social workers. I have talked to peer social workers, senior social workers, and most valuably, newly graduating social workers. These colleagues, in many ways, are the authors of this book.

I don't claim to be a perfect social worker or to know it all. In fact, my training and practice is very psychodynamic. The theory covered in this book is largely derived from history of psychodynamic thinking. This is because I am writing this book from the perspective of my training and my primary skill set. Many fault that, finding psychodynamic theory problematic, inadequately evidence based, and unsuitable for short-term work. The truth is that you can practice with the use of multiple theoretical orientations and still be practicing in a highly clinical manner.

Theory often divides us, problematically. What I hope to achieve with this book is a shift away from that divide. I do believe that we can learn from each other's experiences and practice wisdom. In that spirit, I ask that you let me be your guide as you begin to navigate your way in this profession.

The Paradox of Being New

When I first graduated with my MSW, I knew that I would want to go on to get my doctorate. I knew I was interested in teaching and certainly wanted my terminal degree. I was also panicking that I was not going to get all the information that I needed in two years of school. I have seen that this panic exists nearly across the board. MSW students near graduation are in a highly paradoxical state. For the most part, many feel completely done and saturated. I know I felt that way. They also tend to feel unprepared and scared. One bad supervision experience can leave your training feeling inadequate. It doesn't take much for something to feel off during the two or three years it takes to get an MSW, and this can throw someone into a powerful and fearful state of unpreparedness.

I got lucky with my first job. I was hired in a high functioning college counseling center. I was offered group supervision, individual supervision, and enough clinical hours to receive my next level of licensure. I was also paid a nearly livable wage. Even with all of that, my drive toward a doctorate was clear. So, two years after graduation, I started in a doctoral program that helped remind me of a lot of what I had already learned in my MSW. But it also exposed me to some of the premier experts in the field and offered me models for how I could create my career and how I could think innovatively. Perhaps, most importantly, though, it armed me with a tremendous amount of theory and critical thinking skills that have allowed me to dismantle a lot of the powerful trends that highly influence clinical social work in often fleeting ways. It allowed me, I think, to find my style, my voice, and my way. I got a great job and was able to further my education in seriously satisfying and sustaining ways.

There is a big problem with all of this, though. I have almost $150,000 in student loan debt. I have no idea how I will ever pay that back. Even though I hope this book is a success, I don't think my book royalties will reach that level. That level of debt, for the work and educational experience I have had, does and does not make sense. It makes sense because I know a lot and can teach a lot and think a lot. It doesn't make sense because I simply can't afford it. If you bought this book and are becoming a clinical social worker, neither can you.

I didn't write this book to save you $150,000, but if I can do that, I would be thrilled. I wrote it because my panic about not knowing enough has turned into somewhat of a financial life sentence. I wrote this book because I want you to know that it doesn't have to be that way for you. You can get the knowledge you need on your own. You can find mentors and excellent supervision. And you can do it with real financial and professional bottom lines intact. This book, ideally, will help guide you through theory, decisions about jobs, decisions about supervision, and help you negotiate some of the psychological pitfalls that will come up for you as you find your voice and your way. Most essentially, perhaps, this book will enable you to find ways to allow the field to be your educator. Rather than relying solely on academic institutions, this book will empower you to let your clients and the complex systems that they often function in to educate you. Before investing further, I hope this book will help you assess what resources are around you.

The Bridge From the Academy to the Field

Part of my interest in helping recent graduates identify resources outside of the academy, and within the field, to further their education comes from my own experiences in teaching. First, let me say that teaching new social workers is amazing work. There is perhaps no group of social workers as eager and radical as newly graduating social workers. This is where all the energy in the field is. It is almost always rejuvenating to be in the presence of someone graduating in three months and trying to figure out how to terminate with clients at her placement with grace and benevolent intention. This level of attention and love for the clients is so hard to find in the field after school. It isn't that it isn't happening. It is that it isn't talked about as openly as it is in an educational setting. It doesn't have to be this way, but part of the pressure of the field keeps us from being able to openly discuss the ways in which we are affected moment by moment. I hope that this book provides ideas for creating space for that level of honesty.

Yes, I am interested in moving some of the powerful energy out of the academy and into the field. Furthermore, though, I think there is a problem in a lot of school settings that feels worthy of addressing. What I have found, time and time again, is that there is a problematic divide between educators and the field. Many of the institutions where I have taught have professors tied up with grant-seeking research or grant-funded research. The pressure for grants keeps professors further and further from the complex realities of clinical work. The pressure of professors to keep grants coming also keeps the prioritization of the actual classroom very difficult. This is not what any professor wants, and there is nothing intentional about it. There is simply a crisis in academia overall that is currently perpetuating a large divide between pedagogy and practice.

Part of this divide is bridged by adjunct faculty, like me. I am in the field every day, and I go to teach a day or two each week. I am constantly creating an interplay between the field and classroom. But I have no job security, and for the most part, I am given syllabi that have been around for (in some cases) decades and am instructed to teach accordingly. I have knowledge of the field but minimal power in the academy. This was not the original intention of MSW programs, in my estimation. Although the production of research is essential and moves our work forward, students are often left in the crosshairs of complex political and academic dynamics that compromise their education.

No, this book does not solve that problem in any way. But the goal of it, in some ways, is to create a cross-fertilization between what we learn in school and what we learn in agencies and not to privilege one knowledge set over another.

Reclaiming the Importance of Supervision

One definitive setting in which this cross-fertilization can and should be happening is in supervision. Supervision, in many agencies, has been hijacked by task and administrative discussions that foreclose on the possibility to more fully and richly discuss case conceptualization and theory integration. The field ought to be allowed to serve as a premier educator of clinical social work; however, this education needs the provision of driven and prepared ambassadors. Ideally, these ambassadors are supervisors. But supervisors are often as taxed as professors. Although supervisors are immersed in the field, the pressure for hour by hour, minute by minute productivity is not that different from the academy. And this pressure trickles down and keeps even the most amazing supervisors from knowing and remembering that part of social work was founded on the elegant principle of disseminating practice wisdom. Social work, in many ways, was a field founded on the principle that the elders would educate the youth of the field with practice wisdom that had been attained and refined by decades of diligent practice and thought.

My hope in writing this book, and particularly in the offering of a chapter on supervision, is to reimagine and reclaim the inarguable import of supervision. There is no real way to develop in this field without excellent supervision. A paradigm needs to be recreated in which social workers graduate seeking this vigorously. This supervision ought not to be sought in doctoral programs or training institutes alone. It needs to be a simple and attainable fact of our field. As a supervisor of both groups and individuals who also spends a considerable amount of time in the classroom, I know that there is perhaps no higher form of educational possibility than what can occur between a senior and a junior agency staff member or between two peers in a well-supervised group.

Writing This Book

I said that writing this book was not particularly taxing. It has certainly taken a long time, though. I feel that it is important to say that, because my hope is that born out of this book will be many more books by my readers. The hope, for me, is that the voices of those new in the field are more frequently heard and that the right to write is not reserved for those who have only a specific length of experience. There are many ways to write now—blogging, Tumblr, Facebook, Twitter—but perhaps nothing can replace the staying power of a book that many different generations can make use of over time. There are stories out there about how each of you found your style, your look, your own way of being in the field—and they need to be published. This is partly my story. It is also partly a manuscript that can help you map out your story and to claim your own voice and narrative. There were many times when I wanted to give up on writing this book and had serious doubts about its utility. I have wondered if it has all been said before. Maybe it has, but that doesn't mean it has been said in my voice, and that certainly doesn't mean that it has been said in your voice. And it needs to be said.

It isn't easy to find an editor, and it isn't easy to tolerate the editing process. But the drive to create some sort of a dialogue about what it is really like out there has kept me going, and I hope it will do the same for you. We need to be guiding each other through this field in a way that revisits the days of shared practice wisdom. Without a strong social work community, we are really nothing at all.

My Future and Yours

My ultimate goal in writing this book has been to empower clinical social workers to find a bright and sustaining future for themselves. Many people burn out in social work. Many simply dissociate from the day-to-day pressures of it. Many find that their student loans simply prohibit them from remaining in the field because of the oftentimes nominal financial opportunities. I don't consider myself to be an optimist, but I sincerely don't believe it has to be this way. I do think that the Obama administration has created ways of managing student loan debt, although not enough. I do believe that the endless pressure for productivity deserves some pushback and creative thinking to manage. I do believe that this work can be vicariously traumatizing, but I don't think that means that we need to shut down to manage it.

In the following chapters you will find theory that will help you understand what is going on with your clients and, oftentimes, what is going on in your agencies. You will find ways to manage and take control of your financial bottom lines. You will find ways to understand and harness the intense and often vulnerable feelings that you inevitably develop for your clients. You will gain insight into the different settings where you can work. You will also read about why clinical social work, while a utilitarian tapestry of hand-me-downs, is also wildly unique and stylish in its own *right.*

I also wrote this book in the hopes that other social workers can use it as an energy source to aid in the process of true marathon training. So many of us fall prey to injuries in the sprints we run in the field, when we need to create ways of preserving our internal resources for the truly vulnerable clients with whom we work. They need us to stay powerfully in the game for as long as it takes, to create truer intrapsychic relief for our clients and to work toward societal equality within the systems by which many of them feel oppressed.

Danna R. Bodenheimer
September 2015

Part I

Thinking Clinically

Chapter 1
Introduction:
The Story of Rita

I met Rita in my first-year placement, in a partial day treatment program. There, we connected by meeting on a daily basis. I was exposed to her habits, the stories of her life, her recurrent struggles, and the basic rhythm of her story and symptom presentation. An African American, 55-year-old woman, she struggled with poverty and some health issues commonly related to the urban environ of Philadelphia—asthma and diabetes. A survivor of domestic violence, her central treatment issue became her efforts to protect her daughter from a similar fate. She was fixated on this fear and perseverated around the possibility that her daughter was being hurt by her current boyfriend.

As a treatment team, we did a fair amount of reality testing around this possibility, symptom management, and esteem and empowerment building. I am not sure if these were necessarily Rita's treatment goals, but in a milieu setting, these were the shared treatment goals. I note this lack of clarity, on my part, to both normalize it and to point it out as a phenomenological reality of most of our work. We are told to "meet clients where they are," but are often more guided by value-laden tenets or agency objectives. These include an inherent belief in the value of reality, symptom reduction, linear thought processes, and time-limited treatment. I am not endorsing those treatment goals as problematic, more blindly embedded in how we work without an understanding as to why, or if, they are central to clinical social work practice. At least, that was the case for me, and I imagine that I am not the only one.

Coincidentally, when I was interning at my second-year placement (located about eight blocks from where I was my first year), Rita came in for individual treatment. She had been recently diagnosed with breast cancer, and her oncologist suggested that she seek individual, psychosocial support for the management of this diagnosis. When the case was presented, I volunteered to take it, enthusiastic about the possibility of reconnecting with a former client and about the leg up I would have in already knowing the interior angles of her story. So we continued our work together, somewhat aimlessly. There was the obvious treatment goal of "managing" her diagnosis, but I was not sure that was our clear direction. I am not even sure that a clear direction would have been important, but this particular aimlessness felt more symptomatic of my lack of experience, my less than solid understanding of clinical social work, than of my toleration for the development of a relational bond or ambiguity. I am not even sure what we talked about in those sessions. They were mostly slow, somewhat monotonous, with moments of case management interspersed throughout.

The case management was largely around the breast cancer diagnosis and ways that she could adhere to her treatment, find social supports, and manage her fears. These are important treatment goals, but they were not the thrust of our work together. The thrust of our work together was sort of a weekly haze, although I didn't exactly know that at the time. Instead, I experienced a deep attachment to and sense of responsibility for Rita—so much so that when I was offered a fee-for-service position at this agency, my decision to accept was largely inspired by a wish to remain connected to this one client.

Upon my graduation, our treatment did resume. We re-engaged in our slow dance, unsure of who was the leader or what the dance was we were attempting to master. When it became clear that I could not financially survive with only a few fee-for-service hours at $28.50/hour to be exact, I knew I needed to seek full-time employment. My main fear, though, was leaving Rita. About four months into the third incarnation of our work together, I received an offer for full-time employment. I took the offer contingent on being able to leave early one afternoon a week for my appointment with Rita. When this became too much to manage logistically, I became terrified. I sought out-of-agency supervision to guide me through the ifs and hows of termination.

It wasn't until this meeting that I began to ask myself some important questions. These included questions about what I was scared of and what led me to believe that Rita could not survive without me. The questions only invited more questions. Although the questions were essentially innumerable, I can distill them down to the following:

- What do I believe makes people unwell?
- How long do I think the process of achieving wellness takes?
- Is wellness a reasonable treatment goal? And if so, what is wellness?

- Do I have to go through someone's past to get to make sense of their present?

- Am I in the business of symptom management or symptom relief?

- Do I believe in practicing with a sense of orthodoxy or with a sense of eclecticism?

- What does case conceptualization mean to me?

The answers to these questions, individual to all of us, are threaded into the theoretical weave that substantiates the design of clinical social work.

Although I had certainly been exposed to the theories that may have supported my answering of these questions, sincere application and practice felt like a flimsy endeavor, at best. I was sitting, instead, with three or four deceptively simple guiding principles that served as an approximation for practice guidelines, but that didn't take me quite far enough.

The practice guidelines were loosely organized around the value that "the relationship heals," "meeting clients where they are," and a near fixation on the role of professional neutrality in symptom reduction and that clients have strengths that we need to help them recognize.

I will examine these practice guidelines in both their underlying and apparent content. I will also try to provide more textured answers to the questions, listed above, through the lens of my work with Rita, which often felt more like spelunking than social working.

Chapter 2
The Lens of
Clinical Social Work

The story of Rita illuminates some of the central themes that come up for us as beginning clinicians. These include a fear about our indispensability, a fear of termination, a fear of taking care of our own professional and personal needs, and a dual fear of our own competence and incompetence.

I fell into several of my own psychological minefields in working with Rita. I became convinced of my absolute irreplaceability in her life. It was an ironic position to be in, because I simultaneously felt as if I had no idea what I was doing and that no one else could do my work as well as I could. These moments of sheer grandiosity, coupled with intense doubt, are clinically dangerous for social worker and client alike. The moments also make the possibility of considering a healthy and productive termination all the more difficult. Whatever the opposite of beginner's luck is, is what I had with Rita. As a beginning clinician, you may also struggle to understand your role in the lives of your clients, both the limitations and possibilities of it.

Central to the process of entering the field of social work is a sense of anxiety and confusion. In some ways, that is a healthy and normative part of early career development. However, there are aspects of this confusion and "dis-ease" that are by-products of an educational process that often feels overly generalized.

New social workers often lack specific pieces of knowledge that would make them feel more prepared for the transition from the holding environment of the classroom to the free fall of the field. This book is designed specifically to compensate for that "lack" in the area of clinical social work. Consider this to be your transitional object that will smooth the road from here to there, wherever you decide that "there" is for you as a clinical social worker.

I frequently find when working with students that there is a shared fear that the work they are doing in their field placements isn't "clinical." When addressing clinical issues in class, students will often say, "This is interesting to me, but it doesn't relate to what

I do." A student placed in a hospital might say this, or a student placed at a child welfare agency might say this. In fact, many students placed at schools say this.

You may find varying definitions of clinical social work that are provided to us by different organizations or credentialing agencies. Here are some examples:

According to the California Business and Professions Code (see *http://www.leginfo.ca.gov/cgi-bin/displaycode?section=bpc&group=04001-05000&file=4996-4997.1*), the definition is as follows:

§4996.9. CLINICAL SOCIAL WORK AND PSYCHOTHERAPY DEFINED

The practice of clinical social work is defined as a service in which a special knowledge of social resources, human capabilities, and the part that unconscious motivation plays in determining behavior, is directed at helping people to achieve more adequate, satisfying, and productive social adjustments. The application of social work principles and methods includes, but is not restricted to, counseling and using applied psychotherapy of a nonmedical nature with individuals, families, or groups; providing information and referral services; providing or arranging for the provision of social services; explaining or interpreting the psychosocial aspects in the situations of individuals, families, or groups; helping communities to organize, to provide, or to improve social or health services; doing research related to social work; and the use, application, and integration of the coursework and experience required by Sections 4996.2 and 4996.23.

The National Association of Social Workers' *NASW Standards for Clinical Social Work in Social Work Practice* (2005) incorporates a shorter version of this more comprehensive definition adopted by NASW in 1984:

Clinical social work shares with all social work practice the goal of enhancement and maintenance of psychosocial functioning of individuals, families, and small groups. Clinical social work practice is the professional application of social work theory and methods to the treatment and prevention of psychosocial dysfunction, disability, or impairment, including emotional and mental disorders. It is based on knowledge of one or more theories of human development within a psychosocial context.

The perspective of person-in-situation is central to clinical social work practice. Clinical social work includes interventions directed to interpersonal interactions, intrapsychic dynamics, and life-support and management issues. Clinical social work services consist of assessment; diagnosis; treatment, including psychotherapy and counseling;

client-centered advocacy; consultation; and evaluation. The process of clinical social work is undertaken within the objectives of social work and the principles and values contained in the NASW Code of Ethics.

And the Center for Clinical Social Work (2008) asserts that:

Clinical social work is a mental-health profession whose practitioners, educated in social-work graduate schools and trained under supervision, master a distinctive body of knowledge and skill in order to assess, diagnose, and ameliorate problems, disorders, and conditions that interfere with healthy bio-psychosocial functioning of people—individuals, couples, families, groups—of all ages and backgrounds.

It has occurred to me, over time, that clinical social work is something that must be internally defined and applied. Whatever setting one is in, clinical social work can occur. Arranging for transportation can be clinical social work. So can discharge planning or home assessments. It is a question of how the work is done that ultimately renders it "clinical."

The fact is that "clinical social work" is a term that is subjectively defined. While some believe that clinical social work rests on the premise that there is direct and sustained practice with clients, this is not necessarily the case. Instead, clinical social work is a way of being in the field that renders it different from generalist social work and other clinical modalities—including counseling, psychology, and marriage and family therapy.

Clinical social work is a mindset—a lens. It presupposes that there are certain ways of interacting with people that leave them stronger—that leave them knowing more than they had known about the situation before. These ways of being include: a commitment to recognizing the strengths of our clients, a belief in the transformative nature of the treatment relationship, in-depth assessment practices, and a conviction about the nature of change. Further, clinical social work asserts that central to human wellness is human empowerment—a belief in individual agency for growth, resiliency, and insight.

Clinical social work is characterized by profound and dual attention to both *content* and *process*. There is a set of ethics—tenets of behaviors and thought. There are no limits on specific locations where treatment occurs, time limits set on treatment, or any other set of limitations.

If practicing with these doctrines in mind, clinical social work is occurring. It can occur in an emergency room, a home visit, a foster care agency, or a college counseling center. Clinical social work is a description of an internal experience—for the client and clinician alike—more than an external professional set-up. Further, a seemingly clinical setting is only truly rendered such by the solid internalization of these practice ideals.

Kaleidoscopic Assessment

Among the elements that render clinical social work distinct from other fields of practice is the commitment to view our clients through the lens of a complicated kaleidoscope. The multiple prisms of this kaleidoscope include a unified focus on attachment, trauma, development, and socioeconomics. The synthesis of these elements helps us to create a case conceptualization that ultimately informs the way in which we will practice with our clients. This assessment can take place in the span of an hour-long meeting or over the span of a decade. There is then another lens that becomes superimposed on the kaleidoscope of clinical social work, which is our individual theoretical orientations. These orientations, often eclectic in nature, evolve out of careful thought, substantial experience in school or our own treatment, and often, mentorship and supervision.

Let's go back to the story of my client, Rita. To put Rita under the general lens of clinical social work requires the collection of several important pieces of data, born out of an assessment that ought never be deemed complete. In fact, clinical social work is committed to the notion of evolving assessment, which further delineates it from other realms of practice.

Inherent to a solid assessment of Rita is an understanding of context, and this context involves a basic knowledge of demographics. Rita receives Social Security Disability Income (SSDI), subsidized transportation to get her to treatment appointments, has not attended college, and has never had what she would consider to be a career. On the surface, that is a substantial amount of information. But we also need to know about her neighborhood. Rita lives in North Philadelphia, a low-income, high-crime, predominantly African American neighborhood with a heavy police presence, only one grocery store, and few infrastructure supports. Without substantial knowledge of her community experience, there is no contextual treatment. This is the person-in-environment perspective.

Further, the details of the socioeconomics matter. Rita is on SSDI. But what does that mean in her life? If I am not aware of what that means for her monthly income, I cannot properly address her stressors in the beginning of the month, versus the middle or the end. For Rita, in 2007, each month started with a check of $623.00. By the end of each month, her symptoms were highly inflamed, evidenced by increased moodiness (mainly sadness) and alternating agitation.

Without attention to the role of SSDI, these symptoms could simply be looked at through the lens of diagnosis, and we might identify some signs of bipolar disorder. But with our kaleidoscope in hand, these types of merely diagnostic conclusions become appropriately harder and harder to reach. And that is fortunate, because a central tenet of clinical social work is that we come to genuinely know our clients from the ever-evolving perspective of not knowing. The commitment to collect limitless data keeps us in this not knowing stance, maintaining the client's role as the expert on his or her own life and treatment. Is she manic in the middle of the month, or is she starting to get hungrier? As social workers, we have a commitment to the more human answer to this question, the less diagnostic one, and ultimately the one that might be truer.

When I meet with clients, I now pay close attention to their ZIP Codes. Oftentimes, following a session, I will look up the real estate in that ZIP Code and then in the next ZIP Code over. Why does the next ZIP Code matter? Well, central to good social work assessment is the knowledge about the presence or absence of gentrification in our clients' lives. Clinical social work is committed to the notion that there is an inextricable link between the personal and communal, and central to any communal experience is an awareness of surrounding tensions. Who has resources and who doesn't, and how close are these communities to one another? A person who lives next door to a proverbial dangling carrot is going to demonstrate symptoms. These symptoms can be understood as depression, but they are better understood as oppression, depending on their specific presentation.

Another option, of course, is to go to the neighborhoods where our clients live. Home-based clinical social work is predicated on the importance of this idea. Agency-based and privately practiced clinical social work give us permission to practice without this knowledge. I would argue that we are in the dark without it.

Rita, as I said, does not have the means by which she can get to treatment without the help of a government subsidized transportation system. She cannot afford public transport and does not have a car of her own. In Philadelphia, the government subsidized alternative to public transport is called "Wheels." It is an offshoot of the Department for Public Transportation. Rita often misses appointments or is late for them.

If I were to analyze her through a more traditional psychological lens, I would certainly begin to consider this to be a sign of treatment resistance. I might even consider it to be emblematic of some sort of relational rupture between us. However, one day during my first-year placement, I saw Rita waiting on the steps outside. Group had ended two hours earlier. She said she had called Wheels a few times and that "they were on their way."

Interestingly, one of Rita's central treatment goals was to cease smoking. We would discuss this in group, identify the obstacles, locate points of resistance, and consider possible elements of self sabotage. What hadn't been discussed was that Rita would sit outside for hours daily, after the Center doors had locked, with other patients from her neighborhood who were also waiting for their rides. Everyone outside was smoking. This was simply the form that socialization took in this setting at this time.

Without an awareness of the dysfunctionality of Rita's transportation, I am left considering why she won't take better care of her health and doesn't come to treatment consistently or on time. When considering the role of the transportation, the entire assessment shifts. In fact, her presence at treatment at all is an accomplishment, a triumph over an unreliable system on a nearly daily basis. Her smoking, clearly not good for her physical health, leaves her socially connected in moments of frustration and disappointment. It can even be seen as a healthy mode of self soothing, as it leaves her socially connected instead of isolated.

In other words, clinically informed social work assessment is community assessment. The assessment, even for the individual, must take into consideration the impact of the macro environment, and this impact must be considered in a serious fashion to truly understand the nuances of a client's behavior.

A study conducted at Salem State College demonstrated the importance of poverty when assessing for mental health issues in clinical social work. Hudson (2005) published a large-scale, seven-year study that suggests that poverty, acting through economic stressors such as unemployment and lack of affordable housing, is more likely to precede mental illness than the reverse. Taking into consideration socioeconomics as a significant factor in mental health functioning is ultimately the hallmark of a clinical social work assessment.

Intensifying Assessment Through Attunement to Trauma, Attachment, and Development...or Clinical Social Work Is Trauma Work

Layered on top of astute socioeconomic awareness is our keen attention to the dual roles that trauma and attachment have played in our clients' lives. Attention to the present day macro and micro factors leads us to study the role of attachment and trauma in our clients' histories—histories informed by multiple and complex factors. As clinical social workers, our professional identity assures that we remain tied to the disenfranchised, vulnerable, and underserved members of our population. Given that, it is fair to assume that assaults on attachment and trauma have occurred at a nearly universal level for our clients and that these assaults have somehow disrupted their development. Healthy development rests on the notion that attachment has happened securely and that trauma has not visited us, in either an acute or a chronic, yet subtle, capacity.

As clinical social workers, we do assume that a certain amount of resiliency has promoted development, even rendering the appearance of development as healthy, but stories of development are often quite complicated. Rita was asked to take care of her siblings starting at the age of 11. Her siblings, two boys and a girl, were seven, six, and two years old. Her mother was heavily addicted to alcohol and appointed Rita as the "parent."

As a result, this phase of her development was defined by an incongruence between her psychological capacity and her actual responsibilities. In many ways, to do this parenting, her psyche was forced to play catch up. This process is not one without cost. But it is a cost that we are willing to pay, because the human psyche will pay anything to sustain attachment, even if the attachment is not fortifying. Rita was determined to keep the child care system out of her family's life, to keep her siblings and herself out of foster care. Her attachment to her mother and her wish to remain proximate to her trumped any wish she had to be cared for by another or to shirk her given responsibilities as a surrogate parent.

Attachment often does this—it trumps nearly every other desire. Our work as clinical social workers must be to pay unrelenting tribute to this. This means that every time Rita's transportation was late and she was encouraged during that day of treatment to examine her relationship with cigarettes, what was inadvertently communicated to her was that her wish to self soothe during attachment crises must be changed. Perhaps it did need to be changed, but not without recognition of the gravity of what this shift would mean to her.

Trauma ruptures attachment, and ruptured attachment assails development. To varying degrees, this is true for many of our clients. Assessment without it leads to clinical misattunement, which is actually a reenactment of trauma. Trauma, ultimately, is a dual assault on identity and safety. Thorough and meticulous assessment is the sole way out of this misattunement. It is a head-on look at all that is identity.

When wondering why it is important to incorporate a solid understanding of trauma into our work with clients, it is useful to note that 70% of adults in the U.S. have experienced some type of traumatic event at least once in their lives. That's 223.4 million people. Of those 70%, up to 20% of these people go on to develop PTSD (Rosenthal, 2015). As of today, that's 31.3 million people who did or are struggling with PTSD.

Although, as social workers, we are exposed to an array of diagnoses, I believe there is perhaps no diagnosis as pervasive as PTSD. An openness to that fact keeps us grounded in the realm of work with the oppressed populations we are committed to—populations exposed to trauma through poverty, racism, and pervasive violence and crime.

The recognition of the nearly atmospheric nature of trauma enables us to honor the true vulnerability of our clients' lives. Identifying trauma and treating survivors of trauma brings us face-to-face with our own vulnerability, our own fears in the world, and with the capacity in human beings to, at least momentarily, lose our empathic and human connection to each other, thus making it possible for us to do terrible things to each other. To effectively maintain a solid clinical social work ethic, we must maintain a belief in our own vulnerability, preventing us from the us vs. them dynamic that pervades other more hierarchically informed interventions.

Trauma can result from childhood sexual abuse, as well as other forms of maltreatment during childhood. It can also come from any prolonged exposure to traumatic situations, such as multiple tours of duty in Iraq and Afghanistan. Seeking to identify all the triggers of trauma only relegates our understanding of it as narrow. We are rarely sure of what will have a traumatic impact on our clients, but our openness to the range of possibilities is an honoring of the viral and possibly fatal impact that inequality has upon the human condition.

Trauma has an impact on identity formation in children and sense of self in adults, with profound effects on relationships and self-esteem. Individuals and communities who have been traumatized are often left with feelings of isolation, shame, and a belief in a dim future.

Trauma also leads to changes in self-perception that are characterized by a sense of helplessness, overwhelming feelings of guilt and shame, and a sense of alienation. These changes in self-perception, if understood through the lens of trauma, aid us to feel more prepared to understand human suffering in a particularly empathic manner. Much of our work as clinical social workers is to make sense of why people feel the way they feel. With proper attention given to the role of trauma, many internal states and shifts can be better understood, better empathized with, and better treated.

Also essential to note in our understanding of trauma is the impact that trauma has upon one's system of meanings. One of the central driving forces of our work is to aid clients in the meaning-making process. This may mean that we are aiding clients to make meaning of their symptoms, their grief, their socioeconomic situation, their family histories, their substance abuse. One's loss of meaning can take several forms, including: a loss of sustaining faith or a sense of hopelessness and despair, severe problems with self-regulation, or struggles to experience meaningful affect, vulnerability to depression, substance use disorders, and self-destructive and self-mutilating behaviors. Lost meaning systems also produce fragmented memory and states of dissociation. If trauma divorces one from his or her ability to make meaning, our work becomes focused on how to renew one's relationship with this central element of health and wellness.

Strengths Perspective

The way that we, as clinical social workers, believe that individuals survive the world around them and overcome traumatic life circumstances, is through a solid belief in individual resilience. We also believe that there is an internal human drive toward wellness, though that wellness has varying definitions. The strengths perspective (Weick, Rapp, Sullivan, & Kisthardt, 1989) keeps us committed to the subjective meaning of wellness. What might appear as illness through another theoretical lens can be reinterpreted as strength through this powerful perspective.

Clinical social work begs us to remain not valueless, but value-flexible. In terms of Rita's career, it would be easy to consider her lack of "career" or her minimal education as signs of unwellness. Perhaps we could even consider these factors to be central missing elements in her sense of self. These would be value-laden pieces of assessment. What appears to be a weakness from my perspective may in fact be a coping mechanism at least, or a tremendous asset at most.

Not only are we required to interrogate the very notion of weakness–we cannot be aligned with any one reality. This is no small feat, given that as critical thinkers, our seeking out of a consistent reality is a relentless drive. And our resistance to it must be equally relentless. In this relentlessness, I must reconsider Rita's lack of a career. Perhaps it can be better understood as a wish to remain a constant presence in her daughter's transient life. Having gotten pregnant at 18, Rita's decisions better reflect her unwavering commitment to her family than any failure. Or perhaps her lack of a career can be viewed as a way of staying connected to her mother, who didn't have a career. Given the substantial ways in which she was asked to individuate early and often, her wish to remain identified in this way is one worth valuing and reconsidering.

The strengths perspective requires that we navigate the muddied waters that lie in between cultural relativism and morality. We cannot surrender our moral codes or compasses, yet we are a field guided by a set of ethics. Our morals must be based on the context of our clients' lives, a careful consideration of the impact of stressors upon our clients' minds, and require a certain repositioning of internal geography. This requires us to look more at what is there versus what is not there. This is a tricky stance, given that we are mainly in our clients' lives because something is amiss.

Irrespective of this, our assessments must focus on how much our clients have before assessing what they are missing. It is only with a knowledge of what is present in their lives, what is available to them both internally and externally, that sound interventions can be crafted. The strengths perspective presupposes that all people are filled with an internal reservoir of assets and capacities that have carried them up until the moment they come to meet us. These capacities typically exist in five realms—the mental, physical, emotional, social, and spiritual. Our assessment of one's strengths must include a careful examination of their thought process, their relationship with their body, the ability to feel or their inability to feel (either way providing insight into their ability to adapt), and their formal and informal networks of support.

Through attention to these facets of the self, our unwavering commitment to a client's self-determination is honored. We first assess how self-determination has brought them to this point, and we then work to identify how to maintain and/or increase this self-determination to enhance overall functioning. Simply put, self-determination is a respect for our intrinsic ability to act healthfully and adaptively. Through this lens, what may appear to be wrong choices are a person's attempt to do what is best at the time. It is a solid commitment to the recognition that people essentially do what they have to with what they have, and that given more, more will be done.

The discovery of these intrinsic capacities is the very meaning of empowerment, another central tenet of clinical social work. We encourage our clients to claim whatever is full citizenship in their lives. We encourage a certain entitlement to assume one's rights, one's sense of justice. This empowerment is founded on the notion that our clients have become accustomed to their own oppression and that this oppression has created a sense of powerlessness. The strengths perspective belies the notion that through empowerment, and the recognition of one's own agency, this powerlessness can be reversed.

Given this, solid assessment of the power dynamics present in one's life is central to both assessment and treatment planning. The strengths perspective asserts that individuals have done what they can to survive their own oppression. But it is ultimately through the treatment relationship that more can be done. This perspective posits that through the sheer sharing of stories from client to clinician, empowerment, strength recognition, and reversal of powerlessness can emerge. Inherent in the strengths perspective's view of the world is the significant belief that once a story is told, it can be re-told anew, and that this retelling is a reclaiming of power unto itself.

This perspective, as related to Rita, means that we take what might appear as symptoms or barriers to socialization and understand them through the lens of resiliency. We must maintain the constant conviction that our clients have come quite far without us and that this wisdom must guide the treatment, rather than be treated as pathological phenomena.

Rita is among the few parent figures in her community that remained a consistent attachment figure for her daughter, never engaging in alcohol or drug abuse, ending a domestically violent relationship, and providing adequate food and shelter. Given the obstacles presented to her by poverty and scarce community resources, her life is nothing short of an anomaly. Whatever rendered this anomaly possible is the basis for our understanding of her strengths.

Cultural Competence

The heart of cultural competency suggests that what is true in my community may not be true in yours. Specifically, the very nature of truth is socially constructed and culturally variable. To practice in a culturally competent manner, two central tenets must be honored.

The first is that, simply put, racism and oppression exist. Racism and oppression exist on both macro and micro levels and are transacted through macro and micro aggressions. This means that racism, like trauma, exists nearly atmospherically. The nature of an atmospheric existence is that none of us are immune to its reality, yet it cannot be clearly seen or understood. And, in fact, the elusive nature of the definition and impact of racism is part of what sustains it. We take the ambiguity of the definition of these phenomena seriously, as a sign of their power, not a sign that things are equalizing. Macro aggressions are racial transactions that are easy to see, and the possibility of their powerful impact is a shared perception. Micro aggressions occur more subtly, create a cumulative impact over time, and the presence of them is speciously open to debate. As clinical social workers, we recognize the multiple ways in which racism and oppression operate, honoring both the obvious and subtle by-products of these systems of marginalization.

The second tenet of culturally competent clinical social work is that cultural competence is merely a starting point. Although establishing culturally competent modes of practice is certainly a goal, it is by no means an end. Competence means that we have a rudimentary understanding; it is an adequate or sufficient level of functioning. On one hand, this means that we know we are insufficiently functioning without cultural competence. On the other hand, the goals of adequacy and sufficiency simply aren't lofty enough to align well with social work ethics.

Ethically speaking, the *NASW Code of Ethics* (2008) characterizes that cultural competency is comprised of three elements. The first two are that we are to practice without discrimination against difference and with respect for others. But the third element asks more of us. The *Code of Ethics* states that we should take social and political action.

Clinically, this means that we have a willingness to see ourselves as complicit in the racial structuring of our society while identifying as social change agents who are willing to recognize our own agency for shifting these realities. We cannot possibly recognize the pervasive and viral power of racism while simultaneously seeing ourselves as non-complicit with it. Clinically, we must recognize that racism is a psychic injury and one that warrants repair.

Beyond being competent practitioners, we must also become repairmen and women, recognizing possibilities for social change in any social work encounter. With Rita, this might mean recognizing that her late diagnosis of breast cancer was not a result of her unwillingness to get annual mammograms, but instead resulted from a lack of information given to African American women about breast cancer prevention and care. While treating Rita, I would acknowledge this possibility, seeking to liberate her from the sense that her failing health was her failure. I would also begin to explore the possibility of attending support groups in which she could receive cultural mirroring and support, rather than just suggesting that she go to any breast cancer support group. Perhaps race is an issue for her related to her breast cancer, and perhaps it isn't. What makes the clinical social work with her that I am practicing culturally competent is my persistent, yet not intrusive, insistence that race can always be an issue.

Meeting Clients Where They Are

When we practice clinical social work, cultural competence, the strengths perspective, and attention to trauma are all ways of "meeting clients where they are." Still, "meeting clients where they are" is a term that is used in social work school, both ubiquitously and abstractly. We are here all the time, but what does it mean?

Embedded in the idea of this notion are ideas about the change process, what makes it possible, and what makes it probable. It is asserted, by clinical social workers, that clients cannot change unless they are first seen. In some ways, meeting and seeing are interchangeable. If we try to meet a client on the third step of a building entrance and the client is solidly located on the fifth step, the work cannot start. Not only can it not start, but the notion of having to meet this client is that we are responsible for moving out of our comfort zone before we can request the same of our clients.

Our job is to come to where our clients' psychological cars are parked. This movement, on our part, suggests that we understand that our clients' suffering is requesting enough movement of them. We also recognize that it is only by coming to their parking space that we can make any sense of the real direction out or the obstacles that are in place.

The tenet that suggests that we meet clients where they are suggests that, as clinical social workers, we are first learners before we can (if ever) become teachers. We are the students in the study of our clients' lives, deferring to their expertise. It is from this perspective, as the student, that the change process becomes possible.

This notion suggests that the change process comes in stages and that these stages are not linear and do not look the same from person to person. For the change process to unfold, with or without linearity, solid input from the client is paramount. Ideas about change, about wellness, and about the routes there must be mostly derived from the minds of our clients with some possible aid by our experience. But our experience is secondary to the central belief that change is not an act that can be practiced upon others.

Looking again at Rita, change might mean worrying about her daughter less, securing better financial stability, and achieving a reduction in the symptoms of depression. As a clinical social worker, it is not my belief that these are definitively the paths toward change, or that change can be objectively defined or measured. Instead, I meet Rita where she is.

She is not interested in worrying less; she is interested in her daughter ending her relationship with her boyfriend. I can't make that happen. I can't even suggest that she can. But my empathy can start right there, right on that step. I can experience the devastation of her lack of control with her, and sit with the fear, recognizing the limitations of her agency in the life of a loved one.

For us, as clinical social workers, this is where we meet our clients. This is where change arises—through the mere empathy and toleration of standing on the same step, waiting patiently, and not valuing movement in any one direction over another, but trusting the true functionality of our clients' internal compasses, whose sense of North is heightened by our empathic presence.

The Relationship Heals

All of clinical social work, and what I have mentioned so far, rests on the central premise that the relationship heals. It is our conviction that strong therapeutic alliances, comprised of empathy, provide the lubricant into the inner worlds of our clients. Inherent in the belief in the healing nature of the relationship is an implicit belief in the power of attachment. As clinical social workers, we understand that clients are driven to attach and that this is likely their premier motivator. Without attachment, there cannot be solid motivation for change. It is our relationship that serves as the field though which attachment failures can be remedied; developmental misattunements can be re-aligned; and traumas can be eased by warmth, tenderness, and the resolution to remain present with one another.

Often, students and clinical social workers wonder what exactly they are doing for their clients. This is an interesting and difficult question to ever really answer, yet surprisingly, the underpinnings of the answer are almost always the same. You are building and attending to the maintenance of a relationship. Central to human wellness is the ability to attach, in any number of ways, and our work is to identify the ways in which each client can uniquely attach. For Rita, it might be through smoking cigarettes on the front stoop. For another, it might be composing music. For another, it might be through getting a tattoo that represents a relationship.

When we are unsure of what we are doing, a process of distillation is always helpful. We are assessing and enhancing attachment through the *healing nature of the clinical social work relationship.* The setting in which we do this is secondary to the quality of our relational bonds. And, these relational bonds are only made solid by the acknowledgment of environmental reciprocity between our clients and their worlds and the dual honoring of social justice and individual psyches.

Part 2

Getting Your Theoretical Groove On

Chapter 3
Thinking About Theory

In the story of Rita, I referred to my simultaneous roving and nagging feeling of incompetence and purposelessness. Retrospectively, I would equate these feelings of haziness with a vague sense of theoretical confidence, along with an underdeveloped understanding of what achieves wellness, thereby leaving me unclear of what I was trying to do.

One of the central issues that new social workers, including myself, graduate and grapple with is to identify a comfortable theoretical orientation. Students largely graduate with a generalist sense of the different theoretical ways in which they may practice, but feeling unified with a modality and an orientation takes profound self-searching and savvy. Further, the discovery of a solid theoretical, clinical self often conflicts with the realities of how we are allowed to practice. In the following chapters, I will discuss ways to manage—rather than avoid—these potential tensions. Furthering the use of Rita as a clinical example, I will explore the interrelatedness of theory and technique, while also honoring the distinction between these two entities.

When I first graduated with my MSW, it was with the central goal, as it is for many, to make enough money to survive. Identifying my theoretical lens or clinical belief system was of great import, but it was secondary to survival–and it should be. Unfortunately, and almost uniquely, in social work, maintaining the dual goals of survival and professional refinement can be quite challenging. It is not impossible, though. Through careful attention to a set of bottom lines, a certain clarity can evolve and growth can occur. Some of these bottom lines include a commitment to the *NASW Code of Ethics,* having enough money to eat, and the simple, yet elusive, carving out of a formal internal or external space to think.

It was exactly this space to think that I entered the field without. I had left my placement to return to a summer of classes in late May, with the invitation to return to my field placement setting on a fee-for-service basis. This financial dynamic, for a beginning social worker, can pose quite a threat to the bottom lines I mentioned. It becomes difficult to adhere to a set of ethics when you are literally financially dependent on whether or not your clients show up. Further, the securing of advanced licensure relies on the completion of a certain number of clinical hours, rendering a level of dependence on clients that also can become ethically unsound. It is possible, at a certain point in our careers, that this dependence can be effectively navigated, but not without the clinical fine-tuning that this section will explore. This fine tuning rests on the open exploration of clinical theory.

Psychodynamic and Cognitive Behavioral Theories

Although there are many clinical ways of thinking, it often feels that there are two central umbrellas that theoretical orientations fall under—psychodynamic theories and cognitive and/or behavioral theories. Both agree that the past has an impact on the present. The disagreement comes in how much of a role that can actually play in treatment and how relevant it is to the creation of solid interventions.

Classically, psychodynamic theory has been characterized by the four psychologies: ego, self, object relations, and drive theory. These psychologies have been enhanced by more recent developments in the realms of interpersonal work and, now, relational or intersubjective theories.

Born out of frustration from the lack of measurable results from psychoanalytically informed practice and theory, cognitive behavioral theory and treatment evolved. One more process driven and the other more oriented toward goals and measures, both attempt to relieve symptoms.

Psychodynamic treatment seeks symptom relief through the discovery of the meaning of symptomology and concurrent relationship construction that accompanies this awareness. The empathy provided by the relationship coupled by increased insight paves the way toward wellness or relief.

In the realm of Cognitive Behavioral Therapy (CBT), awareness is heavily valued. This awareness is considered transformative. The focus is on the individual, who through clinical guidance and an examination of internal thought, can achieve self-directed change. Another central delineating factor between these two ways of thinking is that psychodynamic theory is driven by the premise that the unification of affect, behavior, and cognition provides relief. Conversely, CBT argues that mastery over behavior and affect, through the refinement and claiming of power over cognition, provides reprieve.

The following chapters will specifically examine Object Relations, Self Psychology, and Ego Psychology, because of their close symmetries with one another and the similar ways in which they call us to practice. These chapters will be followed by an exploration of Cognitive Behavioral Therapy and its uses in clinical social work.

Other theories exist that are not covered in this book. They include attachment based family therapy, solution focused treatments, behavioral therapy, exposure treatments, motivational interviewing, harm reduction, and dialectical behavioral therapy. This is a less than comprehensive list that attempts to scratch the very plentiful surface of clinical theory.

Chapter 4
Object Relations

Object relations, a theory based on our interrelatedness, was initially conceived of by Melanie Klein in 1952. Although many of the psychodynamic theories that preceded it rested on the notion that the self is an intrapsychic phenomenon, object relations posits that we exist interpersonally. The theory argues that our level of wellness or illness can be measured by the strength and qualities of our relationships. This strength and quality can be measured by the extent to which we have internalized versus introjected our relationships. I will go into the meaning of these words shortly. Object relationists argue that we are driven most by attachment, above and beyond any other internal impulse or wish. Further, object relationists argue that treatment is better informed by an understanding of attachment style than diagnosis, and by an understanding of psychological versus chronological age.

When I imagine object relations, I hold firm to the image of a Thanksgiving table. I ask students or clients to imagine their Thanksgiving table. This is, in many ways, our internal object world. How loud is everyone talking? Is it easy to get to the meal? Do you have to drink your way through it to survive? Are you expecting criticism or love and support, or both? How much food is there, and is there enough? Do you know how much to eat, or do you leave surprisingly stuffed? If you are vegetarian, are there options for you? All these questions are diagnostic measures of one's relationships with his or her internal object world. The term *object* symbolizes our earliest relationships and the subsequent process of internalization of these relationships. Your family members are objects, and your school teachers might be objects. Any attachment figure can serve as an object.

An internal object world, simply put, is our capacity to have taken external relationships into our individual psyches and to hold onto them. However, holding onto them isn't that simple. How hard we need to hold onto them is an essential element of how well we are currently functioning. For those who have a tenuous relationship with their external objects, these relations become represented in the form of introjects. Introjects are two-dimensional representations of our caregivers or loved ones, and they typically exist in the mind in a way that clouds our authentic sense of self, drowns out our own voice, and seeks to narrate some truth about us. Our fear, if we don't listen to these seemingly objective truths, is that our relationship with these objects will end our attachments—that our connections will fail and we will be left alone.

Internalization and Introjection

Relationships that are more sufficiently balanced take the form of internalizations. Internalizations are complex representations of others in our lives, and these complex representations make possible a complex understanding of ourselves. The understanding of ourselves is supported, ultimately, by a chorus of supportive reflections that leaves us the lyricist. If our relationships, instead, are more introjected, we are not likely to be the songwriter or the singer. We are unlikely to have much volume control over the music at all. A formalized term that is applied to our understanding of this is *object constancy.* Object constancy is the basic measurement of how well we can maintain "out of sight," yet not out of mind relations with the important people in our lives. Can we self soothe with the knowledge that even when alone, we have others with us? Is it easy to get to that Thanksgiving meal, and is what we need there? Do we need to binge on it, or is a decent serving adequate because we are well aware that there will be more to eat, metaphorically?

In many ways, object relations maintains that we function in a world of expectancies that are formed by our earliest interactions. Our expectancies are set well in advance of our interactions. Again, to use a metaphor, this feels like a process that is quite akin to the formation of a Microsoft Word document. Upon first opening, the document is completely blank, free of margins, spacing, and fonts. After being opened and manipulated many times, incoming content comes in similarly. If it was saved as Times New Roman, it will open as Times New Roman. If it was saved in 12 point font, it will open in 12 point font. The new writing in the document is saved, but it is dwarfed by the overriding power of the template structure. In real life, how does this look?

For Rita, this can be applied effectively. First, she perseverates on the wellness and safety of her daughter. For Rita, out of sight renders likely the possibility that her daughter will cease to exist. Secondly, Rita's own experience of domestic violence has set her margins in place, and whatever data may be presented to the contrary about the safety of her daughter's relationship is trumped by her experience, which is manifested into the poorly introjected relationship that she holds with her batterer. The relationship with her batterer, of course, was predated by her relationship with her absent mother. This relationship compromised, legitimately, her ability to maintain object constancy. Her mother's addiction made the solid internalization of her as a healthy attachment figure impossible. Instead, she set the stage for Rita to experience relational unpredictability.

Templates for Future Functioning

According to object relations theory, our earliest interactions create a template of interpersonal functioning that defines our lives. The theory heavily favors the impact of attachment as a predictor for future interpersonal satisfaction. As a result, we carry with us a script based on these early interactions and anticipate that present-day interactions will play out similarly to what we have already experienced. The model further posits that we are driven to recreate familiar dynamics in an effort to maintain a sense of familiarity with the world around us. These repetitive patterns are the by-product of unresolved relational conflicts, and also argue for us to stay closer to the devil we know.

Inherent in our understanding of one's object relational functioning is our assessment and understanding of the role that transitional objects play in our clients' lives. When we are looking at their relationships with both people and objects in their lives, we are looking at attachment style. If we have a client who gets a tattoo of her boyfriend's name a month after meeting him, we know something about her ability to internalize this new object. Many clients settle for transitional representations of relationships because the actual internalization of the relationship is just too hard. Or because the road to that internalization is a long one and it has to be paved with objects that symbolically represent that process.

For children, transitional objects are a normative part of development. They symbolize the difficult cognitive and affective task of knowing that your caregivers exist no matter what. A blanket holds a smell. A pacifier offers oral soothing. A stuffed animal holds the experience of softness or tenderness. We look to objects to make the time between the fixes we get from our attachment figures shorter through materials that soothe our senses.

Into adulthood, the transitional objects become more complicated. Clients may need to call our voicemail repeatedly just to remind themselves that we exist. A client might even hold onto a business card to remind him or herself of our presence. I had a client who carried around a picture of me from my website for three weeks prior to calling me. This suggested a good amount about her use of transitional objects and how much easier it was for her to relate to a transitional rather than an actual representation of me.

Transitional objects are not good or bad. We don't view them through a system of values. However, when working through the lens of object relations, we are heavily focused on assessing for the presence, absence, and meaning of transitional objects in the lives of our clients.

Object Relations in Social Work Practice

Object relations gives us effective tools by which we can conceptualize our clients. It also gives us guiding principles for practice. Object relations, in the field of clinical social work, asks that we provide some essential elements. The first is a holding environment. Clinically, this means that we provide consistency within a solid frame. That might mean that we meet at the same time every week, or that we have a quiet space to meet, or routine for how we meet. It isn't the specifics of the holding environment that matter; it is the established reliance and predictability of whatever the environment is. The underlying notion of the provision of a holding environment, particularly in the field of clinical social work, is that it is contrary to the very unpredictable nature of our clients' life experiences. It is the cornerstone of the corrective emotional experience—the second central tool of object relations practice that we seek to provide for our clients.

There is a lot of fear in the field of clinical social work that we don't have enough time with our clients to create any real change. Object relations theory counters that fear with a profound belief in the cumulative nature of corrective emotional experiences that can happen within safe holding environments. If you are working in an ICU and a mother is on the brink of losing her daughter to a life threatening disease, object relations argues that what we can provide in that setting, on that day, can shift the trajectory of the grieving process. The mother can have a place to meet with someone who is willing to tolerate, and not attempt to overly ameliorate, her suffering, in a safe interaction. That can happen in the cafeteria of a hospital or in a private office. The fact is that time is given for the client to feel and that this time, this permission, this space, is curative. It is not curing, but curative. Because we social workers who subscribe to object relations believe that early experiences are predictive and prescriptive, even our tiniest interventions hold power, because we offer the opportunity for new experiences of relating.

If we have the opportunity to go more deeply with our clients in a setting that allows us more prolonged clinical exposure, object relations can guide this deepening. To attend to this deepening, we must consider something about the ego syntonic and ego dystonic nature of our clients' feelings, thoughts, and identities. For something to be ego syntonic, it means that it is comfortably lodged within our minds. For something to be ego dystonic, we are experiencing some discomfort or dissonance around the thought or feeling we are having. The goal of assessing the nature of our clients' ego syntonic vs. dystonic experiences is to get a sense for how at peace they are with their authentic selves versus how at war they are with their authentic selves.

For example, I have a client who is a lesbian, and she is also an Orthodox Jew. When we began seeing each other, her lesbian identity was quite dystonic to her. What she was experiencing as syntonic was a good amount of internalized homophobia and the voices of her particular community, who agreed that her gay identity was "bad." Our work then becomes a process of making the syntonic more dystonic and the dystonic more syntonic. This harkens back to the notion of internalization versus introjection. My client was not able to internalize a true sense of who she was because of the introjected nature of her community. Her community had all of the volume control.

Fortunately, for us as clinical social workers, we believe that one's authentic self pushes quite hard to come through, and we need to join in this pushing process. However, we must carefully join and we must carefully consider what parts of our clients we ought to join with. This is because an aggressive joining, or joining that partners with pieces of a client that frighten the client, will lead to clinical alienation. To properly work with the issues of syntonic and dystonic material, we must clearly adhere to the tenet that we meet clients where they are. However, we are not working from precisely that position—more like a mere centimeter or two away. Every move we make in this work is a measured one, intended to stay close to the client, but not to collude.

As my client became more accepting of her gay identity, her relationship with her family became more dystonic. It is tempting, clinically, to push the burgeoning dystonic awareness further. However, our work as object relationists is to keep our eye on the trump card of attachment. Pushing her growing awareness of her family's disapproval would be to mistakenly push for a particular agenda, which is that having an authentic sense of who you are will lead to wellness. Maybe it does. But object relationists aren't so sure. Having a sense of authenticity is essential, but as clinical social workers, we are required to engage in a case conceptualization that honors our client's object world, attachment history, and sense of self in equal measure.

Object Relations and Attachment in the Therapeutic Alliance

We also believe that all of this has an impact on our clients' interactions with us in the here and now. Object relations theory strongly asserts that the individual is driven by attachment and that without interpersonal relationships, an individual fails to thrive. Although these relationships ought to be supportive and healthy, this is not always the case. We make sense of how healthy these relationships are through an examination of the transference and counter-transference.

Transference is the phenomenon by which we mistake our present experiences for the past, rendering us unable to remain open to new experiences. If I were to ask my client what has gone into her decision to remain closeted versus to come out, she might hear me saying, "Why don't you stay in the closet?" Our work with clients is to unearth their expectancies of how we relate to them and to compare and contrast that to how we are actually relating to them, while creating a treasure hunt back to how they arrived at their original perception. This co-created treasure hunt is the premise of the revelation of unconscious processes—what makes one seemingly blindly assume that things are going a certain way. This treasure hunt also supports the belief that the therapeutic relationship is fertile ground for replaying repetitive patterns of maladaptive behavior or perception. The more the client mistakes us, the more productive our work can be, if we can elucidate these perceptual errors.

Technically, the term for all of this is *reenactment*. As clinically savvy social workers, we remain highly suspicious of invitations to reenact the familiar past of our clients' lives. I might start suggesting that my client move away from her family, but would this be any different from their expressed wish for her to remain closeted, for her to deny herself real love? The fact is that I would be reenacting the role of the objects in her life, which has encouraged her to move away from attachment. It is clinically tempting, and the more fixed the pattern is for the client, the more tempting it becomes for us as practitioners.

Even in the ICU with the mother mentioned earlier, this could happen. It might be that the mother's emotional history was characterized by a series of denials. Every time she cried, her caregivers told her to get over it. She might then say to you, "I really shouldn't be crying to you about this. You need to get on with your work." Those are invitations to reenactments. Object relations theory argues that the cure or the shift comes in the form of refusing or twisting reenactments and replacing them with openness, support, collaboration, and transparency.

While there is no one way to practice object relations theory, it is believed that the power of past interactions can be shifted within the context of the therapeutic relationship, which is viewed as a healing force for change and healthy relational functioning. It is fair to say that the theory posits that present day functioning is a direct product of the past. This present day functioning cannot be shifted appropriately without both proper reflection on the past and a therapeutic relationship that rewires our historical computing. This rewiring is our work, and our work is to introduce and practice new modes of relating and operating—for example, to provide a space where one can wish to attach to his or her homophobic parents, to practice their religion, and to love freely.

Object relations theory notes that "people are constructed in such a fashion that they are inevitably and powerfully drawn together, the reasoning goes, that we are wired for intense and persistent involvement with one another" (Mitchell, 1988, p. 21). We also understand that the personality is a compilation of past attachment failures and successes. Further, our lives are largely guided by an effort to regulate affect and emotions, and we seek to manage our fears and satisfy our desires through our management of attachment.

Object relations lacks pragmatism on multiple levels. The process is lengthy, the training is lengthy, and the theory is esoteric. It also provides us with a way of thinking about our clients that is profoundly aligned with the values of social work. Although many object relations practitioners practice privately and with high fees, it is our work as practitioners (if we believe in this theory of functioning and practice) to cease the deprivation of diverse socioeconomic groups from access to this modality. Offering object relations treatment to socioeconomically marginalized groups would allow for these individuals to truly face attachment crises, histories of trauma, and corrective emotional experiences. This orientation is highly appropriate for clients dealing with long-term and multi-dimensional suffering.

Chapter 5
Ego Psychology

Ego psychology arose in opposition to theories that focused heavily on individual deficits, relational failures, and the process of diagnosis. Instead, ego psychology was designed to honor the many dimensions on which people function and suggests that this functioning must be understood through the powerful context of development.

Freud envisioned the mind as a three-part structure: the *id,* the *ego,* and the *superego.* He argued that the id was comprised of erotic and aggressive impulses. Conversely, the superego acted as a punitive and judgmental administrator. The ego, according to Freud, sought to modulate the competing demands in a way that is aligned with social norms and mature functioning. Ego psychology evolved to understand the ego itself as a much more complex entity than a mere metabolizer of varying drives, impulses, and anxieties. Ego psychology views every individual as having ego capacities and ego defenses. Rather than seeing some as pathological and others as well, ego psychology—well aligned with the values of social work—views us all on a continuum of functionality. We are positioned on this continuum according to both our stage of development and our ability to adapt to our surrounding environment.

Much like social work, ego psychology pays dual attention to environmental influences and inborn potentials. Ego psychology very much subscribes to the notion that there is human resiliency, but that environmental stressors compromise individual functioning. All pathology, or compromised functioning, is understood through the lens of understanding an individual's effort to adapt to his or her own reality. The harder it is for a client to adapt to reality, the more the client will struggle. The practice of ego psychology, as a result, seeks to create a better fit between individual psyche and social environment. Ego psychology argues that failures to adequately adapt happen in the developmental process and must also be repaired developmentally. In other words, ego psychology seeks to identify when a psychological wound occurred before trying to heal. It can only be healed if that developmental piece is honored.

Cohesion and Fragmentation

Ultimately, assessment through the lens of ego psychology takes the shape of assessing for the cohesion versus the fragmentation of the ego. A cohesive ego means that the ego is highly functioning across varying domains, which I will discuss. A more fragmented ego suggests compromised functioning across these domains. This assessment is a huge informant of treatment. The belief is that ego cohesion is the treatment goal and is best achieved through the provision of ego support, which typically takes the form of empathy and validation. More high functioning egos can tolerate more modifying treatment, which often takes the form of interpretation, challenges, and re-narration. All egos can become more cohesive, and the level of fragmentation versus cohesion helps to determine what intervention makes the most sense.

Ego Functioning and Reality Testing

Central to all healthy functioning, according to ego psychology, is the ability to successfully test reality, known as *reality testing*. This is the mind's ability to determine the distinction between what is happening internally versus externally. For psychotic clients, there is minimal capacity to differentiate between internal and external stimuli. These clients would be considered highly fragmented and would benefit from a good amount of ego support, warmth, and non-judgment. Clients who have a more clear perception of reality are considered to be functioning on a more cohesive level of ego functioning. These clients are able to observe the external world without it providing a threatening experience to their sense of self. It is believed that the higher the level of stress or trauma, the harder it is to maintain a solid level of reality testing. Reality testing is vulnerable, because people are vulnerable.

Clinical social work attests to the profound impact of our own vulnerability regarding our ability to perceive the world accurately. The impact of vulnerability on perception is highly aligned with social work values. This is because social workers strongly believe that sustained exposure to poverty, racism, and violence compromises our relationship to the world, and describing this through the lens of reality testing is one of the powerful ways in which we can measure this exposure.

Object Relations as an Ego Function

The second dimension of ego psychology is object relations. Although the term suggests an alignment with object relations theory, it actually posits that object relations are an essential piece of ego functioning, just not the whole of it. In ego psychology, "object relations" refers to our overall capacity for mutually satisfying relationships. An individual with strong object relations capacities can perceive himself or herself and others as whole objects with three-dimensional qualities. A liberating aspect of ego psychology is that one can have poor relational functioning, but still be perceived as highly functioning in other domains. This honors the social work principle that the whole of the person must be considered in assessment. We cannot simply deem people as unhealthy because they do not have substantial relationships. Instead, we would view their strengths and also consider ways of bolstering their deficits. In the case of identifying a problem with object relations, clinical social work treatment would focus specifically on the strengthening of relationships.

Thought Processes

Thought processes are a mode of measuring one's cognitive capacity. Thought processes are expected to be linear, logical, and coherent. Those with highly cohesive egos can tolerate abstract thought, making use of creativity and imagination. More fragmented ego functioning would suggest that individuals struggle with complexity, feel encumbered by disorganized thought processes, and have difficulty thinking conceptually. Again, stress and trauma play a paramount role in our ability to maintain coherent thought processes. Recognizing not just the importance of thought processes, but the vulnerability of these processes, is another way that this psychological orientation is aligned with social work values. Social work, again, adheres to the pervasive impact of oppression and valuing thought processes as variable, subject to stress and tenuous is a way of acknowledging the complex interplay between the mind and the environment.

Impulse Control

Impulse control is our ability to regulate our internal wishes to discharge feelings of aggression and sexual desire. It is also a measure of the lengths to which we go to self-soothe. Some typical examples of problems with impulse control include road rage and intense promiscuity. When linking impulse control with difficulties around self-soothing, we see a different range in symptoms, such as drug and alcohol use or binge eating. Ego psychology believes that we are in need of soothing—that it is inherent to the human condition. How we achieve this soothing is an essential element of how healthfully we function. When assessing clients, we first try to assess whether or not they have the ability to self-soothe at all. This is not an easy element of functioning to assess, and issues in self soothing can often be left out of proper efforts to assess. Someone is able to self soothe if he or she can tolerate a range of emotional experiences, can postpone intense reactions when the social setting calls for it, and has found ways to incorporate the experience of feeling emotion in the life of the body.

For example, a person who becomes quite fearful when speaking in public and might have a panic attack might not accept a speaking engagement. It would also appear that the presence of the fear in the body manifests itself into the feeling of horrible anxiety. For someone who confidently self-soothes, the fear is still there, but the body tolerates it through effective breathing, exercise, and anything else that would allow the person to still speak publicly. The person who does not proceed with the speaking struggles with impulse control, because the anxiety cannot be metabolized, and a self-defeating behavior likely follows. For many who struggle with impulse control, it is fair to say that there has been a failure in the effort to manage anxiety as it enters the body, and that this anxiety is often the by-product of an effort or a failure to self soothe.

Affect Regulation

Affect regulation is one of the most complicated and central elements of how the ego functions. It is a central part of functioning that should be honored in the assessment process and can be aided through the use of good treatment. Affect regulation is the ability to shift between different emotional states without becoming overly anxious or depressed. I am suggesting that anxiety and depression are not actually emotional states unto themselves. Instead, there are places where one retreats when the ability to comfortably manage affect fails. Simply put, there are four core affective states: sadness, joy, fear and anger. Most of our emotional states are at least variations of these base ways of feeling. And experiencing these feelings is not an easy feat to accomplish.

Most of us, when we sense sadness approaching, psychologically flee the scene. We are not comfortable with sadness; it is a difficult way to feel. Often, though, we survive and feel relief once we have experienced it. For those who struggle with affect regulation, that ability to remember that surviving emotions is possible is elusive. Someone who struggles with affect regulation fears emotion and has the vague or strong sense that emotion can annihilate their well being.

Ego psychology posits that the experience of emotion is central to mental health. Further, it can be argued that there are fears of joy and fears of sadness and fears of anger that all exist for varying reasons.

The way ego psychology argues that affect regulation can be better mastered is through the clinical provision of *containment*. Containment is the idea that we provide a therapeutic space for clients that encourages the experience and survival of intense and sometimes frightening emotional states. I often envision containment to look like a jar of jelly. The client is the jelly; the social worker is the jar. For the most part, the clients who struggle with affect regulation feel like jelly and sense that their emotions will break the jar. Maybe their emotions *have* broken the jar. Maybe their anger led them to a rage, and the rage led them to a physical altercation, and now they are unsure if they can survive anger. As a clinical container, or the jar, we offer the provision of the toleration of these emotional states with our mere presence and our willingness to empathize, validate, and reflect back the power of emotion. We provide this jar until the client can reclaim his or her own ability to be both the jelly and the jar.

Judgment

The element of ego functioning that is termed *judgment* is the capacity to act responsibly and according to the basic and reasonable social norms that are expected of us. As social workers who think as relativists, we can find this to be a difficult level of human functioning to assess. We don't want to oversubscribe to any dominant paradigms or expectations about how to "be"—however, we do want to presume that there is some importance associated with our clients' ability to act rationally and predictably when possible. If we have a hungry client, this can be compromised. If we have an unemployed or impoverished client, this can be compromised. In fact, most forms of oppression hurt judgment. Our work as social workers is to examine the impact of this oppression on cognitive functioning, affectual experiences, and behavior. We need to examine this impact, while not holding the client responsible for the ways in which our system has compromised their capacity for strong judgment. Clients with "excellent" judgment can identify possible courses of action, anticipate and evaluate likely consequences, and make sound decisions that benefit the functioning of their lives. As social workers, it is essential for us to note that this is a luxurious level of functioning that can only truly occur upon the provision of basic human needs.

Synthesis

Even more sophisticated and perhaps luxurious than the ability to exercise excellent judgment is the ego's capacity to synthesize, known as *synthesis*. This level of functionality suggests great sophistication and maturity and is often evidenced by the presence of an observing ego. An *observing ego* is one that has the ability to zoom out and observe the actions and thoughts and feelings of oneself. An observing ego allows clients to organize their thoughts and feelings and identity into their personality in a non-disruptive manner. Having the ability to synthesize means that there is some symmetry or alignment between our thoughts, feelings, and actions. It also suggests that we have the ability to tolerate complex and often contradictory pieces of information, experiences, and ideas.

The client who is profoundly nervous about her wedding, yet loves her future partner, will likely tolerate this fear, and she will understand it as symbolic of the process of identity transition and lifetime commitment. This is someone who manages synthesis well. Another person who is terrified on his wedding day and cannot access the information about what led him to this decision and to this day, and flees the scene of the ceremony, may struggle with synthesis. It is not as simple as that, because for some, true synthesis only comes in the moment of actual transition, while awareness and fear about this transition had not been properly managed or metabolized in advance.

Good synthesis happens in a timely manner, but any synthesis is worth welcoming whenever it comes. Poor synthesis simply never comes, and the mind as compartmentalized reigns powerful and supreme.

The Defenses

The ability to compartmentalize versus synthesize can best be described in terms of how the defenses in one's life function. Ego psychologists emphasize the role of defenses and their derivation from early childhood experiences. Ego psychologists also argue that the heavier the presence of defensive functioning, the more fragmented the psyche. A defense is an unconscious (out of our awareness) attempt to protect the individual from a powerful and threatening feeling. Our first defenses develop in infancy and represent our struggle to differentiate between the self and other. These defenses include *denial, projection,* and *splitting.* More mature defenses that deal with ways that we organize our own internal functioning include *repression, regression, reaction formation,* and *displacement.* All adults have, and use, primitive defenses, but most people also have more mature ways of coping with reality and anxiety. Those who do not develop these more mature ways of coping become overly reliant on defensive functioning, and this deeply intrudes upon the solidification of the personality and the self.

Denial

Denial is our amazing ability to simply siphon off a disturbing reality from our consciousness. If we do not want to see our parent as an alcoholic, we simply won't. This is a failure to rectify what is right in front of us. It is a complete failure in reality testing, and it relies heavily on the unconscious to hold unbearable material, which often occurs at the expense of healthy psychological functioning.

Projection

Projection is the assignment of our own feelings onto someone else. For example, I have a client who has long struggled with having doubts about the sustainability of her marriage. She often feels as if there is a sexual deadness between her and her husband. She is certain that they are best friends, but she doesn't know if there has ever really been something romantic between them. She often meditates on this reality during our sessions. At the end of many sessions, she looks at me and says, "I know you think that I should leave him." This is such a complicated position for me to be in, because I am quite engrossed in the pain of the struggle, unclear of which way this should go. But because this level of certainty and clarity feels unbearable to her, she assigns it to me. I could say, "Yes, I do think that," or "No, I don't." Either way, it would not truly reflect how I feel. This is the paradox of working with projection. It often forces us into a corner, because we argue against the projection rather than working together to make sense of the powerful presence of it.

Splitting

Splitting, another infantile level defense, is absence of the capacity to hold two conflicting feelings at one time. If one is having the experience of hating the mother, one cannot also access the feelings of love or softness toward the mother. The ability to hold two conflicting emotional experiences while disallowing either from becoming definitive is a sign of maturity and allows for a feeling of cohesiveness. The inability to withstand conflicting emotions means that only one emotion can get through the door at a time, and when that one feeling is through the door, it becomes defining and eclipsing.

Clinically, this is a hugely significant issue, because we frequently will encounter clients who struggle with splitting. They begin by idealizing us, and when we disappoint them—which we will inevitably do—they start to deeply resent or hate us. Clients who split are simply struggling with issues related to arrested development, where not given the developmental support to negotiate difficult moments of knowing disruptive material.

In the field, we excessively label individuals who split as having borderline personalities. Ego psychology, which recognizes resolution of defensive functioning as a developmental task, asks us to reconsider the role of defenses in diagnosis. Instead, we are encouraged to see splitting as evidence of an early attachment rupture that treatment can ameliorate through consistency and the provision of tolerance for extreme variations between love and hate, idealization and rage.

Repression

Repression, like denial, is the disconnection from difficult material. The difference between repression and denial is that we store the material that we repress on a preconscious level, whereas the material that we deny is stored unconsciously. This may seem like an insignificant distinction, but those who repress can actually access the material they are hiding from without too much effort. For those in denial, the process is much more difficult. To repress is more mature than to deny.

Regression

Regression is the defense that can be best characterized by one's tendency to revisit earlier stages of development. The individual takes on behaviors and tendencies of his or her past. For example, if a child who is well past the potty training stage becomes extremely frightened in the face of separation and starts to have accidents, this can be considered regression. However, the defense is not only about developmental regression; it can also be a regression to past symptoms of mental illness. For example, if a client who has been diagnosed with OCD has solidly evolved an obsession to check the locks on all of the doors, and returns to this behavior in the face of trauma or stress, this can also be considered regression.

Reaction Formation

Similar to repression is the tendency toward *reaction formation*. This is a fascinating psychological phenomenon. The tendency to engage in reaction formation is evidenced by the ability to trade feelings for opposite and more tolerable emotional experiences. This is a significant issue in our treatment communities and often explains a good amount of why individuals who have been abused don't leave their abusers. When a woman is battered by her husband, she might say, "He did it because he had to. He was trying to help me to get better at my job or to toughen me up." The experience of the abuse is there, but our understanding of it is divorced from our psychological and intolerable emotional experience. The woman may be horribly hurt by the pain and by her batterer's ability to hurt her. Rather than engaging in that sadness, the woman reverses the story and subsequently hopes that her emotions will shift in accordance with the cognitive switch she has made. This emotion often doesn't switch, though, because emotions are often great signifiers of truth. What happens with the original emotion is that it typically becomes directed inward or displaced, another defensive function.

Displacement

Displacement is the misdirection of anger or feelings from an original object onto another. For example, if the battered woman were to hit her child when she got home, this would be an act of displacement. She is actually angry with her husband. She is hurt, and she can't manage it—and she has a less powerful object to displace the feelings onto. We often see in families that struggle with domestic abuse that there is abuse from the children onto the family pets. It is precisely because of a cycle of reaction formation and displacement that this phenomenon manifests itself.

I am not addressing all of the defenses here. Rather, I am noting the ones that hold the most value for us as clinical social workers. These are the defenses that we see in traumatized clients and oppressed clients. The presence of alternate defenses is certainly possible, but it is essential to have these readily available in our toolbox of interpretation and assessment.

Wellness and the Ego

Ego psychology posits that wellness comes from the recognition of defenses, the notation of their limitations, and a consistent highlighting of strength and adaption. This occurs through the provision of insight and the encouragement of the tolerance of affect through the containment that our work provides to our clients. We aim to offer ego cohesion through ego support, validation, reflection, and accompaniment on difficult emotional journeys that lead to solid levels of mature development. This is a highly strengths-based model that is emblematic of true holistic assessment, refusing to deduce a client to a diagnosis by finding shortcoming in one area of functionality or an overreliance on one defense. Instead, we seek to create autonomous ego functioning free from psychopathology, and we recognize that this process can only occur with true tribute to the continuum of individual functioning within the environment.

Chapter 6
Self Psychology

Self psychology, another psychodynamic framework through which to consider the psyche, holds strong alignments with the values and tenets of social work. Key to the practice of clinical social work is a near marriage to the idea of self-determination. Self psychology echoes this sentiment exactly, arguing that the healthy self is a self that is vibrant, creative, loving, and cohesive. Self psychology posits that the self is the center of human functioning, but that the self can only evolve out of relationship. Without both dyadic functioning and the presence of community, the healthy self cannot grow.

The Self

Contrary to earlier beliefs about the driving forces of internal conflict and impulses toward sex and aggression, self psychology states that self is constructed from the inside out, rather than the outside in. Furthermore, self psychology argues that self is truly developed in accordance with efforts to manage and make sense of rejection. Self psychology believes that the notion of the "self" exists on a continuum. There are several ways of describing this continuum, but essentially, health is measured by how true versus false our sense of self is. Or, we consider wellness to be the achievement of self actualization versus the persistent and nagging feelings that accompany a fragile and empty self.

To truly internalize the meaning of the self, through the lens of self psychology, is a complex endeavor. The self is many things—it is partly identity, partly a social construct, and partly a by-product of multiple interpersonal relationships. The development of the self evolves out of symbiosis and mirroring with primary caregivers. What this means is that an emotional life cannot properly evolve without actual emotional reflection.

When a child falls and scrapes his knee, his caregiver can respond in many ways. In order to aid in the development of the self, though, the most useful way is to remain as attuned and open to the authentic experience of the child as possible. A parent or caregiver can say, "Don't cry. It is no big deal." That, symbolically, would have an impact on the formation of a child's own understanding of his or her emotions and internal experiences. That would dominate the language with which the child can begin to understand what is happening. The child on an instinctual level feels the pain, and on an intellectual level hears the caregiver's narrative of the pain, and is left with a compromised emotional response that does not accurately reflect the actual experience.

This notion, that the power of accurately attuned mirroring helps to develop solid emotional lives, is nearly identical to the social work ideal that we meet clients where they are. Although the language is slightly different, the ideas aren't. As social workers, we are committed to remaining close to our clients, not just because this is what we are told, but because this is what fosters the development of a sense of self.

Self psychology evolved out of extensive research on mother-child interactions. The less engaged the mother, the more likely the child would be to attain an insecure identity, which is best described as the vague sense of not being "real." Many clients struggle with believing themselves, their own stories, their own suffering. This is exactly because their experiences lacked the appropriate narration and reflection. Clients who struggle with dominant feelings of falsehood tend to attach themselves to powerful figures, groups, movements, or even substances. The feeling of not quite being real is one that requires constant negotiation and soothing, through often destructive means.

Twinship, Idealization, and Mirroring

It is believed that three central needs have to be fulfilled for a true self to become solidified. These are *mirroring, twinship,* and *idealization. Mirroring* is the literal reflection of one's experiences in the mind and experience of an other. *Twinship* is the need to identify pieces of one's identity in others in order to make good sense of oneself. For example, a young gay boy growing up in a community where everyone is identified as heterosexual is never offered the twinship he needs to figure out his own identity. Twinship gives us language, a sense of possibility and modeling that leads us to believe that who we are internally can safely be exhibited externally. The coming out process has shifted to earlier developmental stages. This is because we are finally in a time when twinship opportunities are making that phenomenon possible. *Idealization* is the final piece of the puzzle that solves the mystery of the self. Without objects that we can readily idealize, the ability to become whole is compromised. This calls not only for the need for role models, but also for the experience of safe naïveté. We need to believe in (at least for a time) the invincibility and wisdom of those who take care of us. There needs to be a phase in our lives when we experience strong feelings of safety and security. It is only from within this position of security that the self can grow. Feelings of safety bred by idealization are the fertilizer of our ultimate ability to best negotiate danger and disappointment.

In 1977, Heinz Kohut wrote that our sense of independence and our belief in our own initiative is most alive when we are most integrated with our most central ambitions and ideals. Kohut suggested that the self is the organizing principle of personality and behavior, and that self is achieved and constructed through the process of transforming positive healthy objects into an internalized self structure. This self structure helps us to weather the storms of life (Stepansky & Goldberg, 1984).

In Treatment?

So how is self psychology performed, and how does this happen specifically in the realm of clinical social work? Given the complexity of the theory, the intervention is quite simple and happens in the form of accurate and highly attuned provision of *empathy*. Interventions in self psychology do not rely on interpretation or the wisdom of the practitioner. Like social work, self psychology argues for a non-hierarchical structure in the work. Interpretation suggests a powerful knowing on the part of the social worker— instead, self psychology asks us to use vicarious introspection. *Vicarious introspection,* as defined by Kohut, is a form of empathy that involves the analyst's attempt to understand the patient from the position of the social worker's own emotional world and history. We seek internal experiences that are aligned with what our clients describe and cultivate empathy through the position of equality and understanding. The client cannot be understood until the social worker searches within himself or herself for self knowledge, awareness, and tolerance of multiple feeling states.

Further, we engage in the effort to validate and affirm the growing and evolving selves of our clients, open to their evolution rather than rejecting of the inevitable shifts of the human condition. We also allow our clients to experience a certain merger and likeness with us, allowing for a twinship experience, to help patients identify how they are both alike and different from those to whom they attach. It is through attachment that this awareness becomes possible. Further, the experience of essential alikeness with another human is the core ingredient in the quest to experience realness. Our work with clients through the lens of self psychology is to allow for the growth and development of an internal world through positive interpersonal experiences. We recognize the toll that misattuned, violent, or oppressive experiences have on the psyche. We recognize that shared emotional moments and empathy provide for profound correction and grounding.

Chapter 7
Cognitive Behavioral Therapy

Strongly evidence-based and practical, cognitive behavioral therapy (or CBT) offers a concrete way to work with clients' suffering. Rather than dealing largely in abstraction, as called for in many of the psychodynamic theories, CBT attempts to make the abstract both transparent and measurable. Founded by Albert Ellis and Aaron Beck after years of frustration with a lack of clear results from practicing psychodynamic theory, CBT has always been concerned with outcomes. Although there are multiple forms of CBT being practiced today and the number is only proliferating, the focus on symptom reduction and a focus on the "here and now" of our clients' lives unite all forms of CBT.

Psychodynamic theory argues that relief from pain and suffering comes at the hands of experiencing synchronistic affect, behavior, and cognition. It is argued that it is through this very alignment that change can occur. In significant contrast to that notion, CBT suggests that through studying of our own thoughts, we can change our behaviors and feelings. CBT works with clients to cultivate a certain mastery over thought processes, eliciting insight and changes in actions following insight development. In many ways, CBT is misperceived as lacking an insight base. Although CBT does not rely on insight in the same way that psychodynamic theory does, meaning that there is not a careful and studied focus on the past, insight is still the path toward change.

CBT is organized around the development of three central capacities: coping skills, problem-solving abilities, and cognitive restructuring. CBT asks the client to develop an ability to observe one's own thought processes before reacting to the content of one's thought processes. It is the effort to cultivate an ability to observe one's own internal processes before those processes are demonstrated externally that underscores the drive behind CBT interventions.

Schemas, Cognitive Distortion, and Automatic Thoughts

CBT was originally conceived of as an effective treatment for depression. In recent years, though, its applicability has been broadened to anxiety disorders and even psychotic disorders. When Aaron Beck originally conceived of CBT, he believed that individuals suffering from depression were suffering at the hands of a tripartite negative view of themselves, the world, and the future. He argued that we function out of cognitive schemas, which are frames of reference through which we interpret all events and experiences. If our schema is negative, then incoming material will be encoded as such.

Further, CBT argues that thoughts cause feelings, and behaviors result in reaction to these feelings. It is ultimately the meaning we associate with these thoughts that is at the root of our psychosocial dysfunction. As CBT practitioners, we encourage clients to become students of their own thoughts. This study begins by encouraging clients to identify their typical thought processes and to then label them as part of an overall way of thinking. The major depressive thought patterns that are identified by CBT are the following:

- I am inadequate, ineffective, incompetent, can't cope.
- I am powerless, out of control, trapped.
- I am vulnerable, likely to be hurt, weak, needy.
- I am inferior, a failure, not good enough, defective, don't measure up.
- I am unlikable, unwanted, will be rejected or abandoned, will always be alone.
- I am undesirable, unattractive, ugly, boring, have nothing to offer.
- I am different, defective, not good enough to be loved by others, a nerd.
- I am bad, irresponsible, worthless.
- I am dangerous, toxic, evil, inhuman.

Upon recognizing one of these patterns of thought, the student or client must come to recognize several possible ways that the power of these thoughts becomes sustained. This is through certain forms of thinking, which include *catastrophizing,* or assuming the worst of all possible outcomes. For example, if one is to fail a test, one is certain to feel that he or she will also fail the entire course.

The task with a client with depressive tendencies is to begin to think in more manageable and realistic terms about the outcomes of experiences that feel frightening.

All or nothing thinking is another mode of thinking that compromises one's ability to feel in a way that is tolerable and in keeping with the reality of external stimuli. The form that all or nothing thinking takes, for example, is when a client has just started dating and experiences the first pang of a doubt or a question about the viability of a relationship. When experiencing these commonplace feelings, waves of panic and sadness follow, because the feelings definitively mean that the relationship must end. It is the inability to view emotions, or any other data for that matter, as signs of ambiguity and greyness that confirms one's tendency to subscribe to all or nothing thinking.

Cognitive-behavioral therapy subscribes to the notion that we are harmed by our submission to emotional reason, otherwise known as the "if I feel it, it must be true" state of mind. CBT argues that emotions create cognitive distortions, and that our emotions ought not to create automatic thoughts. These automatic thoughts, theoretically, leave us stuck in thought patterns that are debilitating. These thought patterns also are what keep us most unhappy and stuck.

CBT is typically brief and time limited. The number of sessions is often agreed upon at the commencement of the work. This forces a certain level of productivity and economy during session. The average number of sessions is 16. During those 16 sessions, sometimes fewer, the client and practitioner work collaboratively to focus on current behavior. In the collaboration, the client is responsible for the definition of goals, expression of current concerns, and the effort to implement and internalize the work in between each session through homework and constant exercises associated with the treatment. The therapist helps the client to define goals, listens, encourages the client, and points out notable, problematic thought patterns. The therapist also teaches the client about strategies that can be used to better master his or her own internal processes.

The therapist or social worker's role further expands to educate the client on the benefits of remaining calm when faced with difficult situations. Clients are asked to practice and eventually strengthen their capacity to experience a problem, observe their own feelings about the problem, and then to carefully determine a course of action. CBT practitioners urge clients to subscribe to rational thought and to rely on facts rather than assumptions. In many ways, this may sound very similar to the scientific method that we were taught in grade school, and it is. The belief is that hypothesis testing must be implemented before assuming the veracity of any perceptions and taking any actions associated with these perceptions.

A CBT-oriented therapy session is structured and focused on the already stated goals, and it works to remedy the problem of lacking skills or coping mechanisms to properly manage stress. CBT is based on the assumption that most of our emotional and behavioral reactions are learned by association and that we have been trained to maintain our belief in these associations. The goal of treatment then becomes an unlearning process. Let's look at an example of how this unlearning can occur.

Unlearning and Re-Learning

I have a client, Jacob, who recently spent Friday night alone. His experience of this was quite positive. He cooked for himself, trying out some new recipes, and watched a movie. When we began treatment, Jacob's negative feelings about himself were deeply intertwined with his negative schema about the world. He oversubscribed to several cognitive distortions, which included the belief that he was not well liked, not attractive, and was physically awkward. To start to dismantle the embeddedness and near reflexiveness of these thoughts, we first needed to identify the etiology of this schema, to reveal its origins. This is not about creating a fixation on the past, but simply an effort to make sense of how current perceptions are the by-product of past associations.

Jacob was not a particularly "cool" kid in school, according to him, and perhaps that was the case. He was frequently chosen "last" for dodgeball and was often asked to do math homework for his peers. He did many of his friends' homework in an effort to be liked and connected socially.

During the early sessions of work, it is central to collect data on the client's thought patterns. This data was collected during our first three sessions. Upon this collection, it is the therapist's role to explain how negative cognitions contribute to current distress. The explication ought to support the exposure of an internal blueprint that has supported the current mental scaffolding that is holding the mind together.

The way this information was collected and this blueprint revealed, in our work together, was through conversations that are organized through a structured interview. It also occurs through the client's commitment to homework. To expedite the process by which CBT is performed, homework is a central feature of the work. This is also because CBT is largely substantiated by an ethic that the treatment rests largely upon the client's own independence, rather than dependence on the practitioner. I could have worked with this client to help him develop the insight that would illuminate the narrative of his childhood. Instead, I asked him to pay attention and record between sessions the building blocks of what appeared to be his "automatic" thoughts.

Upon recognizing these building blocks, or the materials through which these beliefs became constructed, our work is to "reality test" the current strength of these beliefs. We begin to wonder how these beliefs "hold up" against current fact and circumstance.

When discussing Jacob's life, we were able to identify several contradictory findings about his present life that weakened the grasp of these preconceived notions. This work is done during the middle phase of our work together. This phase is characterized by the client's effort to better assess, identify, and evaluate the impact of his negative thoughts and to replace these thoughts with alternate thoughts or hypotheses. This is the phase during which the therapist is the most collaborative and active. During this time, the client and therapist co-study and test the logic of each negative thought that passes through the client. The focus then shifts from the examination of thoughts and their associated repercussions to the development of new coping skills and problem-solving capacities.

Through the comparison of current data with past beliefs, Jacob came to notice that his beliefs were archaic, ineffectual, and essentially irrelevant. He is highly educated, socially connected, and quite successful professionally. He also has a great sense of humor, evidenced by feedback from friends, family, and me.

His new behaviors are now informed by different beliefs and assumptions. Had he been without social plans, on a Friday night, when our work started, he would have felt depressed and alone. The lack of plans would have confirmed his cognitive distortions about his general un-likeability, and he would have spent the night self-sabotaging in some way. This could have meant that he would have binged on four pizzas, that he isolated himself for the remainder of the evening, and that he sought to collect data that further confirmed his negative schema and cognitive distortion that was frequently sustained by all or nothing thinking: "If I don't have plans tonight, then I will never have plans again."

He is feeling newly aware of the possibility that the past is the past, the present can be fulfilling, and the future has some promise. Given these realizations, one night alone is now experienced as an opportunity, a reprieve from his active week, and a chance to explore his culinary interests.

CBT in Conclusion

The final sessions of CBT are dedicated to the solidification of gains and planning how to avoid recurrence of depressive or anxious mood states. Because CBT is based on the assumption that the realization of our maladaptive cognitions can help us shift into healthier behaviors, it is also important to note what was blocking this realization process and to clear the path for it in the future. This phase is largely supported by the idiographic data that is collected in the treatment.

Implicit and predominant throughout the CBT process is a system of tracking symptoms. Patients track their own symptoms, note their own sense of improvement or symptom reduction, and have this data to revisit in the future as a near transitional object of the work that has been done collaboratively.

Designed to alter how we construct reality, CBT requires reflection, documentation, and the serious consideration of alternate possibilities to what we have come to know as "true." CBT values individual responsibility for this irrationality, and an individual effort to shift the irrationality. As a result, the client/social worker relationship needs to end to allow the client to practice these new abilities.

Social Work and CBT

CBT has some alignment with social work values. First of all, it is both pragmatic and highly results driven. It is accessible to clients who cannot afford long-term treatment. Seeking to devalue the power of thoughts by ridding them of their associated meaning, CBT is a deconstructive process that builds and is sustained by the development of critical thought. Critical thought, or the importance of self-study, is endemic to the practice of clinical social work. CBT is also focused on solving one problem at a time, leaving clients to feel that each problem they experience deserves its own level of attention and focus.

There are also very realistic limitations to practicing CBT with the disenfranchised populations that social workers are committed to serve. First, it requires a certain level of literacy, because of the homework that is required. This is a literacy that many of our clients simply don't have. Also, while it might be very productive to focus on one problem at a time, it might not reflect the reality of how suffering manifests itself in our clients' lives. Problems are often difficult to parse out. More often than not, they coexist. Finally, CBT relies on the possibly mistaken assumption that clients have the time to complete homework and assignments that this modality requires.

Chapter 8
Burning Questions and Case Conceptualization

So you have a bag filled with theories. Now what? What theory do you pick out of the bag? Is the right theory for you even in the bag? Can you mix and match theories?

The way to begin to answer these questions is with a series of other questions, oddly enough. These questions are the ones I asked myself in my work with Rita. They are:

- What makes us unwell?
- What do I believe makes people well?
- How long do I think the process of achieving wellness takes?
- Is wellness a reasonable treatment goal?
- Do I have to go through someone's past to make sense of his or her present?
- Am I in the business of symptom management or symptom relief?
- Do I believe in practicing with a sense of orthodoxy or with a sense of eclecticism? Maybe I feel a predominant loyalty to an orientation, but I find that I am flexible when the situation calls for it.

Ultimately, all of these questions boil down to one thing: *case conceptualization.* No matter your setting or the parameters of your work with a client, it is essential to cultivate a solid case conceptualization. Without it, our work lacks infrastructure, rendering it flimsy and subject to whims and wind. Case conceptualization is our effort to make sense of a case, and to begin to answer the "why" questions about how our client is functioning.

Case conceptualization has multiple elements within it. These include honoring of the role of socioeconomics; paying attention to the presence of diagnostic issues; and having an understanding of family history, the impact of health problems, and the presence or absence of coping skills. In our case conceptualization, we are required to ask ourselves what is limiting the possibility of our client functioning more fully. So, let's look at each question individually.

What makes us unwell?

Of course, the answers to this question are infinite in number, and I cannot begin to provide all of them. Being guided by certain beliefs about suffering and how it manifests itself is quite helpful in any clinical social work you do.

Social work, as a lens, provides some universal answers to the question. On a fundamental level, social work is heavily subscribed to the notion that inequality and oppression perpetuate unwellness, specifically through the oppressive mechanisms of racism and poverty. Some other possibilities of what leaves us unwell include: ruptured attachments, the inability to self-soothe, a fragmented sense of identity, cognitive distortions, developmental misattunement, long-term exposure to violence, acute experiences of trauma, failed interpersonal relationships, family of origin issues, the overdevelopment of a false self, and the underdevelopment of an authentic self. Unwellness could also be the by-product of struggles with realistic and accurate perceptions of reality, or an overreliance on the idea that life functions according to binaries that render the human experience of ambiguity unbearable. What appears to be nearly unilaterally agreed upon across the theoretical constructs that inform our work is that a lack of insight leads to diminished functioning, leaving us unable to understand our motivations, our internal worlds, and the reasoning behind our actions.

Let's take a look at an example of how to apply the question about wellness to a case. A 28-year-old Pakistani woman, who is a filmmaker, has returned to her home country after receiving six years of university level education in the United States (both bachelor's and master's level). We will call her "Sumi." She is married to a man, but he lives in Canada, where he does his work. She recently produced a film on the history of rape in Pakistan. She is receiving multiple honors, internationally. She comes into treatment complaining of serious issues with depression, as evidenced by exhaustion, a lack of motivation, frequent crying spells, and relief only brought on by self injury—mainly cutting on her arms in a way that inflicts minor wounds. She is surrounded by her family of origin, who are not educated in the ways that she has been, and who refuse to see her film. She feels socially isolated and marred by the psychological experience of feeling as if she is "without a home." During college, she experimented with her sexuality and had sexual relationships with women. She ceased this immediately upon graduation, for fear of how her family would react.

I am sure that as you read this, many ideas came to mind about what is "wrong" or leaving Sumi feeling "unwell." In many ways, the issues are obvious, but it is our responsibility as clinical social workers to apply a theoretical understanding to our burgeoning insight. We must do this, because the theory that we develop will guide our treatment.

If we were to hypothesize that Sumi is struggling with feelings of cultural alienation, then we would clearly be subscribing to the belief that pressures to culturally assimilate take a psychological toll, and that the struggle of immigration and reintegration can lead to symptoms. The very notion of symptoms would suggest that we believe that our psychological experiences make themselves known symbolically. For example, she is self-injuring. Unable to process the pain in an adequate manner within the confines of her own mind, the pain is inflicted upon her body. The very notion of symptoms also suggests that psychological issues require processing in order to liberate one from diagnostic level functioning. We know that not talking about how she is feeling is leaving her symptomatic. We hypothesize that talking about how she feels may lead to resolution. That is a belief; it is a belief about the value of connection, about the value of articulation, about the relief that is provided when one moves from the internalization of struggles to the externalization of them.

If we are to begin to examine that she is feeling confused or dissatisfied by her current sexual identification as heterosexual, then we are assuming that identity matters and that the performance of an inauthentic identity is ushering in pain and discomfort. To agree that identity is a central piece of wellness becomes a key directive in our treatment. It becomes a target area to which we must pay precise attention.

It isn't that we begin to assume that she is gay and living as a straight woman. Unwellness is rarely relieved by the provision of simple answers and insights. Instead, we need to become deeply curious about her sexuality, her relationship with her husband, how she felt in college versus how she feels now, and whether her wish to remain in a heterosexual marriage is one imbued by her wish to survive within her current cultural context or a true reflection of love she is feeling. Either way, the answers she will arrive at won't be right or wrong. They will simply be hers. Our joining her in her journey to answer difficult questions is the work of shifting unwellness to wellness. It is not the content of the data that we collect, but instead our authentically curious wish to collect it. And it is our subsequent accompaniment on the road to finding answers to what our clients experience as unsolvable mysteries.

What is interesting in the example is that there is a substantial amount of manifest (or obvious) content that might leave us feeling confused about the fact that she is depressed. She went to school to become a filmmaker and is experiencing profound success doing so. However, in our work as clinical social workers who are committed to solid case conceptualization, we must never be fooled by what is superficially apparent. It isn't that superficial data isn't valuable. It is invaluable. But it is truly rendered invaluable by our effort to make meaning of it.

Why did she produce a movie about rape in Pakistan? The asking of these questions starts to illuminate the essential role that understanding trauma plays in case conceptualization. In fact, no case conceptualization is complete without meticulous attention to the role of trauma. Was the movie inspired by her own experience of trauma? Is she feeling any trauma at the hands of having been exposed to all of the material she studied to produce the movie?

Trauma does not need to be acute to be impactful, and it does not have to match our traditional understanding of it. The broader our definition of trauma can become, the better able we are to recognize its psychological operations. For this client, trauma may simply mean the overexposure to external stimuli that burdened her psychological ability to process that material in a reasonable and timely manner. The fact is that we can never be conclusive about the role of trauma in one's psychological functioning, because its role is evolving by definition. Awareness of the evolutionary nature of trauma's impact on the psyche is a central piece of any solid case conceptualization.

Some other issues related to unwellness are immediately brought to mind here. There is a very central and straightforward issue of one's need for a support system. This support system can be comprised of like-minded or quite different individuals. The central premise of a functioning support system is that it is merely accepting of the nuanced personalities within it.

Does this client appear to have a solid support system? We know that her partner is far away, that she feels intellectually mismatched with her family of origin, and that she felt frightened about continuing to explore her sexuality in her post-graduate life. This suggests some level of compromised function in this system's ability to keep her afloat. At the same time, she was drawn home for a reason, and this reason is likely substantially correlated with attachment. When conceptualizing attachment as clinical social workers, the role of attachment must be present on our radar screens. Who are her attachments to? How do they make her feel? Anxious? Comforted? Invisible? Visible?

The brief vignette could be examined for chapters on end. This is just the surface. But it is also the beginning of a case conceptualization, and in this brief case conceptualization, our treatment guide begins.

What makes people well?

Social work does a bit to answer these questions in a very broad manner for us, and then it becomes our job to uniquely personalize the answer for each of our clients. Social work agrees that the very idea of treating someone holistically, in a way that honors his or her bio-, psycho-, and social functioning, is curative. Further, social work relies upon the solid construction of a therapeutic alliance to move the work forward. Social work also supports the notions that the self ought to be experienced authentically, that wide ranges of affect ought to be comfortably tolerated, that inequality is a route toward illness, and equality is a route toward wellness, and finally that it is important to simply be "seen."

With those guides solidly in place, our job then becomes moving into more specificity for each of our clients. In other words, our work requires us to move forward with a certain sense that we know what we are doing. We need some objectives in place. Paradoxically, though, we also need to go forward with a decent amount of "not-knowing" in place. This balance between knowing and not knowing is central in our effort toward cultivating wellness, because it suggests that we use our education and training, yet remain deferential to the expertise and wisdom of our clients. This mere surrender and deference in itself is a presumed step toward wellness, because allowing our clients a sense of authority in their own lives, particularly in the context of a preconceived hierarchical relationship (that between the social worker and the client), is reparative. It acknowledges previous disempowering structures of their social and institutional relationships, and it attempts to right this wrong with the provision of a new and corrective emotional experience.

We must also determine whether we are in the business of creating dependence or independence in our clients' relationships with others and ourselves. This is not a simple decision to make, and we are never solidly sure of it. With the aforementioned client, the question has to be answered through a solid assessment of her current relational functioning. Does she feel safe when she needs to be dependent? Is dependency a risk she can even take? Is she independent in a way that leaves her untouchable and unknown? Has she experienced interdependence? These questions lead to particular interventions. If she struggles with dependency and begins calling me, her social worker, every day, we are clearly not headed into new and possibly healing territory. Maybe she needs to do that in the beginning of the relationship to make it feel familiar, but to relate in that way over a sustained period of time would merely be an enactment.

As social workers, we are very interested in the role of enactments in treatment, but not in merely compliance or observance of them. When we recognize an enactment, we must both allow for it and create alteration in it. I might say to this client that she is welcome to call me, and it might also be interesting for her to try—one day a week—to make decisions on her own. We would then take the opportunity to explore all of the sensations related to that risk taking.

You might notice that I am not suggesting that she never call me. This is because a lot of work takes the form of harm reduction. This is not a commentary on how we treat substance use disorders. Instead, it is that endemic to social work is a true recognition of the time that it takes for the change process to occur, and that for real change to happen, gradual steps must be taken. Wherever people are in relationship to their own feelings of independence must be accounted for in the structure and evolution of the therapeutic alliance. The ultimate goal, if it can be simply stated, is for one to tolerate the coexistence of the self and the other. The self and other can and often do coexist. But they don't require full merger or extreme isolation for each to survive. An alternate way to put language to this element of the treatment is to understand that we are in the business of ego construction, and solid ego construction cannot occur without a careful examination of what is already in place. You can't build a house without a foundation. Yet, you don't need to build a foundation if one is already in place.

The wish to construct solid egos, through the provision of containing and reliable boundary setting, is another central piece of the wellness puzzle. Much of our work is exacted by our commitment to and adherence to a practice framework. This frame might mean that we meet for 50 minutes a session or 15 minutes. This frame might mean that we meet in the same place every week, with the same furnishings and same window treatments. This frame might be that we always have cold water available or that we do or don't shake hands upon meeting. It is the consistency and structure that we offer that paves the way for the trust that ultimately enables the possibility for change in our clients' lives.

There is no one way to understand why this is true, but one way to understand it theoretically is that our clients need containment. Containment, or the provision of a holding environment, is a concept that powerfully informs our work. There is a belief that unwellness is sustained by feelings of internal and external chaos. Through the provision of predictability, reliability, and consistency, we are providing our clients with the fertilizer necessary for some new roots to grow.

Content and Process

Another tributary that makes its way toward the river of wellness is the idea of how to manage content and process, or content versus process. We want to spend a good amount of time examining and talking about our clients' lives; however, we also want to help them to develop the capacity to talk about how they think about their lives. We want to equip them with reflective capacities that ultimately leave them more in control of their choices. The reason we attend to both content and process is because it is important for people to understand what motivates them, what informs the choices they make (good or bad or both), and for them to be able to have insight into the patterns of their lives.

Let's say we spend a 45-minute session with Sumi, and for the first 30 minutes of the session, she is talking about all of the accolades she is getting for her film. We might make the suggestion to move away from the content of the session. It isn't that we want to stop hearing her; it is that we want to create an environment where we can also hear what is behind her words. This might look something like, "I am learning so much about how your movie evolved. I wonder how it feels to be sharing all of this." Or, "This is such a fascinating story about how your movie came to be. Have you had the opportunity to share this with anyone else?" We are still evidencing an interest in the content, but we are also making a move toward understanding the underlying process of the content.

Making shifts like this, from content to process, is what makes a conversation therapeutic rather than pedestrian. These interventions, slight archaeological excavations, have to be well-timed and well tolerated. The stronger one's sense of self, ego cohesion, object relatedness, or grasp on reality is, the easier these interventions are to make. The more fragmented and disorganized a client feels, the harder it is to do this. And that's okay.

The other route through which we can move between content and process is through the use of the technique of *interpretation*. Interpretation is a potent therapeutic intervention. In many ways, it is overused and underestimated. Rather than asking Sumi how it feels to be sharing all of this information about her experience, an interpretation would sound something like: "You are sharing a lot of information about your recent success. It sounds like this is a dynamic that you have expressed comfort with before. Perhaps you are trying to make me provide you with the approval that your parents won't provide for your achievement." This is a slightly heavy-handed version of an interpretation, but it is also a very clear demonstration of how content can be transformed into process.

Getting interpretation "right" is no small feat. And encouraging clients to tell us when we are wrong is one way to manage the frequent mistakes embedded in the effort to provide interpretation. An interpretation made in a way that is informed by clinical social work would almost always be prefaced by, "Please tell me if I am wrong," "This is just a guess," "I am getting the feeling that... but you would know better than me." We need to offer our interpretations in a way that allows them to be metabolized. Interpretations offered with a false sense of confidence or an unearned sense of authority can prove to be extremely destructive to the therapeutic alliance.

Further, clients without truly strong senses of self will take our interpretations as truths. This is also quite dangerous, because it is not our goal to replace their internal sense of not knowing and chaos with our sense of knowing. We are trying to replace their internal sense of chaos with their own internal sense of knowing. Conversely, though, a well-timed and accurate interpretation can make a client feel held and contained in a way that few other interventions can. Essentially, interpretation is always available to us. The goal is to use it sparingly and to use it well.

In between validation and the mere questioning of process are several other tools that are quite efficacious in the effort to transform a conversation into a therapeutic one. These tools include *validation* of one's experiences—simply articulating back to them what is clearly there. If a client has been robbed, we might validate them by saying, "Of course that was terrifying. How could you have not been afraid?" This is in many ways the most superficial route toward moving content to process, pedestrian dialogue to therapeutic dialogue.

Next is the tool of *reflection*. This is slightly more intense than validation, because you are reflecting back what the client is showing you that she might see. Sumi might be talking about her wish to remain distant from her mother, and our work would be to help her–through reflection–to see what potential affect states are part of her cognitive experience. "I hear you saying that you might be angry and that the distance is your way of demonstrating that." It is an interpretation, but a mild one, because it takes off from exactly where the client is.

Clarification asks clients to dig deeper into the content they are presenting. By the act of questioning and sincerely seeking clarity on what is presented, we are asking clients to delve deeper into the contours of their own minds.

There are two underlying forces that make any of these interventions work, or make these interventions effective, and those are the essential forces of curiosity and empathy on the part of the clinician. If interpretation is verbal transaction, then empathy and curiosity are the currency by which this transaction is made possible.

The notion of *diagnosis* is another fraction of this equation. Some would argue, in more medical model driven modalities, that diagnosis is simply what guides treatment. Social workers believe that to a point.

An easy example of how diagnosis guides treatment is to think of a request by a client to read his or her file. Let's say one client, John, has paranoid personality disorder and the other, Andrea, has borderline personality disorder. These differing diagnoses would lead to differing responses. For John, the paranoid client, this might be an effort to connect and the only way that he feels the treatment can move forward. For Andrea, this might be an effort to disrupt the treatment, to perhaps act invasively, to be demonstrating a level of distrust that is just qualitatively different from paranoia. I might show the chart to one client immediately and discuss it in depth with the other first.

With Sumi, considering her diagnosis of depression would certainly guide treatment. It would be symptom focused. Social work treatment is symptom focused, but it is also more. I am interested in her symptoms as related to her diagnosis. I am also interested in her attachment history, her cultural experience, her development, and her struggles with trauma. I am wondering if her symptoms are the by-product of all of these issues that can be termed diagnosis or can be termed complex human functioning. This is a classic example of "both/and."

The Role of Trauma in Developing Wellness

And what about the role of trauma in the development of wellness? Does treating trauma mean talking about trauma? Does it mean revisualizing it? Does it mean that we make meaning of it somehow? Does it mean that we help our client to seek justice for it? Every trauma is treated differently, but social work essentially searches to allow for the integration rather than the dissociation of trauma. Inherent in our belief, as social workers, is that a siphoning off of psychic experience is more destructive, though sometimes necessary, than the ultimate toleration of that experience. Was Sumi's movie an effort to extract trauma from her mind, to make meaning of it, to seek justice for it? The point is to try to find out and to work toward the survival of past trauma rather than the fleeing of psychological states that prevent us from our past, present, and future.

So, wellness is a lot of things. It might be the reformulation of insecure attachment into secure. It might be the integration of trauma into the mind rather than the dissociation of it. It might be the solidification of identity. It might be the recognition of oppression and racism and the psychic wounds inflicted by these violences. It might mean that a client achieves mastery over his or her mind, or it might mean that surrender to one's internal struggles is in order. It might occur intrapsychically, and it might occur interpersonally.

The answers to these questions can only be found in solid case conceptualization, with the help of the client and through our careful confidence to both know and not know at the same time.

Transference, Countertransference, and Wellness

Somewhere in all of our thinking about what transports someone to a place of higher functionality are the dual notions of transference and countertransference. Although these concepts are most located within psychodynamic thought, they lend any practitioner, in any orientation, a useful way of thinking about the dynamics that are at play and meaningful in the treatment relationship.

Transference is all of the material that clients bring from their past into the treatment relationship and transpose onto current encounters. For example, Sumi, our filmmaker, may have faced a tremendous amount of rejection from her family in the past for efforts to individuate. I might have to call her to cancel a session, or I might even yawn during a session, and she would receive this communication in two ways. The first is that she would recognize that in the here and now, I am tired or do need to cancel the session. But attached to the perception would also be the potential feeling that she was boring me, that I was angry at her, or that I didn't want to see her. Transference and awareness of reality are not mutually exclusive. They do muddy each other, though.

Countertransference is the psychological phenomenon by which the social worker's past intermingles with the social worker's experience of what is occurring or being transacted in the present. I have a client with whom I have a tremendous amount of countertransference. I mostly experience this in the form of my fear that he will terminate with me. I have been seeing him for more than six years, and not a single session has gone by without my feeling as if this is his last session. Perhaps I am picking up on something from his own attachment history or his own ambivalence about our work together. But to practice in a truly egalitarian and social work minded manner, I need to at least consider that this is my "stuff," and that these are my "fears" from my own life. I need to acknowledge that there is something about him that sets off something in me that is linked to my own psychological history.

These examples of transference and countertransference are not bad; they simply "are." The presence of the complex emotional moments of interplay is only bad if they are underutilized and/or denied. The denial of their presence will likely thwart any treatment. Clinical social work is not the realm in which we seek to leave much unsaid. Instead, the key is to first accept the existence of their powerful presence and then to attempt to make use of the psychological forces that are present at the hands of transference and countertransference.

How do we make use of these forces? That is one of the central treatment questions that has informed much of the writing on clinical practice for decades, if not centuries. I am going to try to talk about this in a very accessible way.

The first step that makes the possibility of using transference and countertransference possible is to make its presence transparent. Let's say that you sense that a client is perceiving a reaction from you that doesn't feel true to how you are actually feeling. One option is to say, "I wonder if something familiar is coming up for you right now," or "Is this is a way that you have felt in relationships before?" The goal, though, is to not make clients feel pathologized for their perceptions and to make sure that you are not suggesting that their experience is something that is happening entirely in their own heads.

The reason it is so important to make transference transparent is that part of what leads to emotional turmoil is a lack of clarity as to what is happening in the present versus the past. Extreme emotional turmoil is often the direct by-product of experiencing the present as if it is the past. Allowing clients the opportunity to differentiate by questioning the possibility that their sense of the here and now is diluted by the haunting nature of the past can lead to profound liberation. It is creating room for the mere, yet exquisite, possibility that "that was then" and "this is now."

A more clinically sound way of wording this is to say that we allow clients to have emotionally corrective experiences. A client anticipates a dynamic unfolding in a particular way. We both highlight the power of that very expectancy and offer a twist to the outcome. Simply put, we dapple in reenactment by exploring what the client was anticipating and offer a twist—a new experience.

Of course, this isn't simple at all. The presence of transference is both difficult to alter and necessary for positive treatment in many clinical encounters. Conversely, extreme transference can be quite debilitating to treatment. A client can come in and feel problematically overwhelmed by the familiarity that is triggered by whatever the clinician brings. This doesn't render the treatment impossible—just more difficult to manage and potentially more rewarding, because the opportunity to resolve huge aspects of what is currently blocking someone's ability to take in new data, new stimuli, and new relational experiences is all the more powerful.

Countertransference, a phenomenon long considered to be a deterrent to successful treatment, is increasingly becoming viewed as an invaluable clinical tool. Every clinician—every social worker—experiences countertransference. That is just how it is. It would be impossible to come into clinical encounters as the blank slate that clinicians were once expected to be. Our countertransferential responses are composites of multiple psychological experiences, including what our clients bring up for us from our own pasts, what our clients induce in us that they aren't fully dealing with, and pieces of unconscious material that are present in the room. These pieces of material might have originated from our psyche or from the psyche of our clients or from something that has been co-created in the treatment relationship. The value of countertransference is not necessarily found in the perfect etiological search of its roots, but rather in the successful attempt to make meaning of it in treatment.

Countertransference in Action—An Illustration

Let me illustrate. I had been seeing Alicia for several years before we decided to terminate because she was moving across the country. It was a complicated termination, because it did not feel particularly tied to an organic ending within the treatment relationship, but to an external need to honor geographical limitations and a professional opportunity for her husband. When Alicia returned to the area, I was curious about whether or not we would resume treatment. She would contact me intermittently to update me on her life, but with no mention of resuming treatment.

She finally e-mailed me with content that felt more appropriate for therapy than for e-mail. I decided to say something, which was quite scary, because I was stuck on the perception that she did not want to resume treatment. I wrote, "I wonder if the issues you are bringing up would be easier to discuss in the context of therapy and if you would like to come in for a session?" Waiting for an answer, I felt incredibly vulnerable and shy.

I am putting this out there because these are important, common, and powerful countertransferential responses. They are also uncomfortable. Further, it is essential to point out that it is nearly impossible to determine where these feelings are originating. Is it because I was chosen last for dodge ball in second grade? Is it because she doesn't really want to resume treatment? Is it because she does and doesn't know how to say it? Am I worried because I don't know if I was a good enough social worker for her? The answer: yes, yes, yes, and yes. It is all of these things.

We did resume treatment. She e-mailed back well over a week later and said she would like to come in on an every other week basis—an ambivalent resumption, to be sure. Several sessions in, she stated that she was having an incredibly difficult time reconnecting to friends locally and that it just seemed that no one was interested in the fact that she was back in town, resuming her life here.

This felt like an important opportunity to make use of the complicated countertransference that I had been experiencing in our effort to reconnect. I stated the following: "I wonder if I can tell you a bit about my experience and if it would help at all. When you returned to town, I was very much looking forward to reconnecting, but I had no idea if you were interested. Even when you did communicate with me, I had a very hard time determining what you actually wanted. This could largely be my own stuff, but I am really not sure, and maybe we could figure it out together." She was astounded to hear about my experience and stated that she had only held back because she didn't want to burden me or my schedule.

By sharing my own intrapsychic experience with her, Alicia got some potential insight into why she was having the general social experience she was having. She gained insight into how her own fears about her worth to others keeps her from demonstrating any vulnerability, leaving those around her feeling all the vulnerability and desire for closeness. I never stated that my countertransference was her fault. I put it out there for us to co-explore and make sense of, all while remaining vigilantly open to my own role in the perpetuation of the uncertainty and insecurity that I was experiencing.

This is a route toward wellness, through transparency, sharing of insight, and the shared exploration of how patterns of emotional relatedness evolve in our clients' lives. We only have our own experiences of our clients, and the more generous we are in our efforts to carefully and constructively study these experiences with them, the more we pave the way for growth. We remove blind spots by holding up different angles and reflection of our clients in the world.

Is wellness a reasonable treatment goal?

The question about what constitutes wellness is naturally followed by a query into the possibility of actually achieving wellness. Given that wellness is individually defined for each client, the answer to this question ought to truly be "yes." However, the answer is only "yes" if we are open to the evolving nature of how wellness becomes subjectively defined.

For example, I had a client who came in to discuss the recent loss of her brother to suicide. Let's call her "Cassandra." Her goals were specific—to begin to feel her grief. Taking a history of her life, wellness could have meant a lot of different things. Her relationship with her brother had been profoundly complicated; her relationship with her parents was also less than optimal. She described her family as organized around the management of her mother's emotional life and that everyone else's emotional experiences were secondary to that central family principle. The more my assessment with her unfolded, the clearer it became that she had multiple significant life stressors happening at one time. In addition to the disturbing loss of her brother, she felt utterly lost in life. She had a stable job that brought her no satisfaction at all. She knew she wanted a change, but had no idea as to how to go about achieving this. When we would discuss the possibility of change, the therapy stopped. It felt downright halted, uncomfortable, and stifling. However, when discussing her brother, the therapy came back to life. She was engaged and loved to talk about him. We discussed his tastes in music, his favorite books, his opinions on religion, and more than anything, we discussed the suicide itself, in depth.

When we talked about her brother, Cassandra cried, sometimes laughed, and was incredibly thoughtful. Moving away from that subject rendered her silent, frustrated, and disconnected.

So, what is wellness with her? And was it achievable? Cassandra very clearly articulated what wellness at this time would mean to her. It would be about grieving her brother. Could it have meant more things? Sure. Did her feelings of being professionally adrift or alienated from her family suggest that the definition of wellness could have been broadened? Yes. But she didn't broaden it.

It isn't that we can't see broader visions of wellness than our clients have for themselves; it is that those visions cannot preempt or trump the information that is right in front of us, what is clearly being spelled out. The fact is that in relationship to wellness, we are in a very tenuous position. It is our work to "see," to offer clarity, and to meet our clients where they are. That is akin to being in many places at one time.

Cassandra ended treatment by e-mail. Perhaps this in itself is a sign that wellness was never achieved. Perhaps the content of the e-mail suggests that we ended exactly in the place she wanted to land.

This is what she wrote:

I just wanted to let you know that I won't be coming in this Wednesday. After having a break for a few weeks, I've come to the conclusion that therapy is not currently a necessity for me, and I think it makes more sense for me to focus my time, energy, and money on other endeavors.

I hope you know how much you have helped and taught me, and how grateful I am. I truly appreciate your patience and kindness, and perhaps most of all, your understanding of Brad as a person and his role in my life. I'm sure he would have liked to know you.

Thank you also for your compassion and gentleness. Opening up to a stranger was something I wasn't sure I would be able to do, but you put me at ease and never made me feel threatened or judged. Sessions with you were, as far as I can tell, as close to painless as therapy gets, and I feel very lucky to have found you.

Believe it or not, I think that this e-mail says everything about wellness that we need to know. Was it achievable? Somewhat, yes. She connected, she grieved, and she shared her brother, promoting the possibility that her memory of him can live in my mind and hers, and it does. The e-mail also suggests a true adherence to her original treatment goals. Our respect for the continuing staying power of those intentions is the central path toward co-achieving anything even proximate to wellness with our clients.

Do I have to go through someone's past to make sense of his or her present?

Although discussing one's past often brings tremendous relief, it can also produce quite a burden. Many people feel intruded upon by thoughts and images of their past, and talking about this material can lead to profound discomfort. The goal, of course, is not to avoid that pain associated with talking about difficult material. But the question we have to ask ourselves as clinicians is, "Do I have to go through there to get where I think my client needs to go?" Sometimes, yes, you do. But what is painfully beautiful about the human mind and how it operates in treatment is that the mind finds a way to make what needs to be known, known.

Many issues that clients have sublimated from their past will find a way of getting themselves worked out in the present. I have a client, Diane, who came in to her first session telling me what her mom said the fee should be. She was 25 at the time, employed, and financially independent. I was concerned about going with this, but I also knew that given that it was a reasonable fee, there was important clinical material to be unearthed in this. We could have talked for sessions about all of the decisions her mother has made for her. We could have talked about the primary role her mother plays in many of her relationships. These would have been and still can be very, very useful dialogues. But these dialogues are also not the sole route toward success. Not every client has access to a plethora of memories, and many lack insight about those memories. Still, change is completely possible.

Over time, we began to talk about Diane's budget, how much she thought therapy should cost, and what she perceived she could afford. We talked about her budget a lot. I didn't tell her what her budget was; she told me. She informed me of her expenses as she had come to know them. Although we were never overtly discussing her mother, we were in a way talking about her the whole time. We were also twisting how things usually go by my allowing her to guide the dialogue about money through her own self-knowledge and experience.

After several weeks of debate and observation of her financial situation, Diane set a new fee for herself. It was $5 more than the original fee her mother had stated she could pay. Does this mean she is cured? No, of course not. Our work is never that simple. But was she able to make an important shift without extreme efforts to excavate painful material? Yes. The material still presented itself, but in a form that she could metabolize and that we could work fruitfully on together.

Part of our tasks as clinical social workers is to identify how material makes itself available, even when cloaked or subtle. Most clinical encounters are clinical opportunities. Our work is to tune in to truly hear each of their unique presentations.

Am I in the business of symptom management or symptom relief?

This is a nearly impossible question to answer without the help of a client in front of you. But the fact is that different theoretical orientations are aligned with different goals. While the more psychodynamic theories are interested in symptom management, the goal is certainly more oriented to long-term symptom relief. More behavioral and cognitive oriented theories are interested in the management of symptom relief.

It is simple to subscribe to symptom relief, a longer-term goal, because it is seemingly the loftier of the two. However, without proper symptom management, the relief may not be possible.

First, let's distinguish between the two. *Symptom management* is the effort to reduce the intensity of current symptoms, to loosen their hold on daily functioning, and to provide clients with the coping skills necessary to manage the advent of recurrent symptoms.

Conversely, *symptom relief* seeks to rid someone of symptoms over the long term. Some might argue that symptom relief requires the increase of symptoms before true relief can come. When a practitioner is interested in long-term symptom relief, a certain onslaught of symptoms needs to occur to truly understand the symptoms and make sense of their meaning. When a practitioner is interested in symptom management, the immediate interest is in ridding the client of the symptoms in a quick and efficient manner.

I don't want to falsely dichotomize these goals, but I also want to aid you in your effort to clarify your intentions. In this effort to clarify your clinical intentions, your relationship with your clients' symptoms becomes clearer. If you are more interested in long-term relief, the presence of intense symptoms won't make you feel as though your treatment process has become diverted. Instead, it will be a welcome (though frustrating and overwhelming) part of the treatment process. Symptoms will sometimes signify growth and sometimes signify regression, but their presence will be part of your work.

Of course, there are certain symptoms that we are unequivocally in the business of both managing and ultimately relieving. These are symptoms related to suicidality and dangerous levels of self-injury. When working with clients, we are required to assess their symptomatology in a hierarchical manner, prioritizing those that are most dangerous. Many symptoms are uncomfortable, but not all are dangerous. We must create this distinction through careful study and observation.

Some symptoms are dangerous, some are irritating, and some are frustrating and unrelenting. Our work, as clinical social workers, is to figure out our position in relationship to the many symptoms that affect our clients' lives and to determine exactly where our responsibility lies in the ultimate diffusion of the hold that symptoms have.

Do I believe in practicing with a sense of orthodoxy or with a sense of eclecticism?

We are often presented with the flawed notion that we will find a theoretical orientation and stick to it. This is rarely the case, even though the notion is sustained in countless ways. First, most websites for agencies or mental health practices identify themselves with a theoretical orientation. It is part of how our work is branded and promoted. Some agencies assure symptom relief through a 12-week manualized program, while others argue that the provision of psychodynamic treatment is the sole way forward. The issue of practicing with a sense of orthodoxy is further promoted by the way in which insurance companies expect progress notes to be written. Many insurance companies ask that we treat in a problem focused, symptom reduction, time-limited manner. Recent research on evidence based practices further pressures us to identity a form of treatment that "works" and to stick to it.

The fact is that the push toward orthodoxy or brand loyalty is a move away from client-focused treatment. The more theories we know and the more tools we have in our toolbox, the more likely we are to design a treatment that suits the individual needs of the client in front of us.

When speaking about my client, Jacob, who suffers from low self esteem and had created a long standing narrative of his unlikeability, cognitive behavioral therapy lent a helping hand in forming both a solid case conceptualization and subsequent interventions. When speaking about Sumi, the filmmaker from Pakistan, I never applied any language that relates to CBT and instead formulated the case through a more object relations/ego psychology lens.

The distinction here is both meaningful and meaningless. It is meaningless because the differences between theoretical orientations are largely linguistic constructs. They are sets of different words to describe very similar phenomena. Essentially all theoretical orientations are interested in hypothesizing about what leads to suffering and have ideas about how to change it. Are the actual hypotheses that different? I don't think so. Getting overly attached to one language over another leaves us without the amazing ability that being multilingual gives us to articulate our perceptions in precise and textured ways.

It is also paramount to remember that all of the theories and interventions that we study were created by individual people. Yes, the people were smart. But these are also people who had minds of their own, traumas of their own, quirky families of origin, or trouble sleeping, or felt anxious or depressed. The theories were born out of imperfect minds, and although that is largely the beauty of them, it is also a serious liability if we become overly indoctrinated by any one way of thinking. The theories are valuable ways of thinking, and that is all they are. The more eclectically we are open to practicing, the more minds we are honoring from the history of our field.

Continuums, Binaries, and Wellness

Contrary to the suggested idea supporting this chapter, I have found it quite useful to reconsider the ideas of wellness and unwellness as falsely dichotomized notions about how we function. When practicing, I have found it considerably more useful to think about human functionality along the lines of several continuums. These continuums liberate me in my thinking about case conceptualization.

The use of continuums, conceptually, also liberates clients in profound ways from thinking along the lines of binaries that no one actually falls into. The ending of binary thinking enhances our ability to think about our clients and to aid our clients in better understanding themselves. It is a move toward wellness, unto itself, by agreeing that we all function along very textured mutations of gray, honoring our individuality and connectedness at the hands of this reality.

Annihilation Versus Engulfment

It is my sincere conviction that intimacy is a universal struggle. Although it may be a largely shared desire, it is simultaneously a discomforting prospect for many. In fact, it appears that human functioning is nearly driven in equal parts by a fear of and a wish for intimacy. I share this with my clients, and it often brings substantial relief. We have been indoctrinated by the idea that intimacy is healthy and that ambivalence about it is pathological. I wonder, though, if intimacy can even truly exist without some level of ambivalence.

When theoreticians were originally conceiving of the underlying struggle of the schizophrenic mind, it was posited that schizophrenic patients were embroiled in an intrapsychic war between two opposite poles, each representing a fear. One pole is the fear of annihilation, and the other is the fear of engulfment. Presumably, the schizophrenic mind experienced the possibility of intimacy as possibly terminating individual existence or representing complete merger. I would argue that on some level, these fears exist within all of us. While we are kept afloat by our wish for closeness that leaves us related to one another, there are aspects (although minute for some) of all of our psyches that fear that we will either be engulfed or ended by closeness.

Awareness of the pervasive nature of these fears allows clients to feel somewhat normalized in their very complicated interpersonal experiences. Further, noting that these feelings exist for many on a continuum frees us from over-diagnosing the presence of these psychological experiences and simply accepting that they are part of the human condition.

Fear of Joy Versus Fear of Pain

Embedded in the acceptance of this continuum is the reality that we experience fear of joy and fear of pain in similar measure. We have come to classically understand that if fear exists, it is a fear of pain and discomfort. That is often the case. However, there is also a very real, common, and legitimate fear of the experience of joy. This is because with joy comes vulnerability, and not just vulnerability about the temporal nature of joy, but vulnerability that comes with the very experience of joy, which requires a surrender of inhibition and a certain level of abandon to truly experience. Recognizing this reality offers clients a way of better understanding their own avoidant tendencies, promulgating the notion that fear is part of both happiness and sadness and not always a sign that something is wrong.

The normalization process of the complex ways in which emotions make themselves known to us aids clients in the process of accepting their own internal experiences of how things actually feel, rather than fixating how they should feel.

Feminine Versus Masculine, Gay Versus Straight

The Kinsey Scale was first published in 1948. Yet, a solid understanding of the gradations of how gender and sexuality are experienced still eludes us. Alfred Kinsey, an expert on sexuality, posited that we all exist somewhere on a 6-point scale between heterosexual and homosexual, with bisexuality existing in the middle. Freud ascertained something quite similar, hypothesizing that 80% of the population is bisexual, 10% is gay, and 10% is heterosexual. These numbers are useful, but first they only address sexuality. Secondly, they still suggest that each individual holds some empirical value that is equated to a definitive state of sexuality. Clinically, I have found that individuals do struggle with identifying their sexuality. There is also an unrelenting internal struggle to accept the very fluid nature of how both sexuality and gender are experienced.

The fact is that both sexuality and gender are experienced in extremely complex ways. Gender is rarely felt in one way over time, or even in one way throughout a day. Our experiences of our gender identities twist and turn throughout our lifetimes. However, great distress occurs at the hands of not experiencing gender in prescribed and prepackaged ways. Treating clients along the lines of the reality that these continuums exist, and that our experience of ourselves evolves incessantly, frees them from the constriction of binary expectations that society prescribes for our experience of ourselves.

Abundance Versus Scarcity

When creating a case conceptualization, I like to try to position my understanding of a client according to where his or her experience with scarcity versus abundance falls. Perhaps this is a more nuanced understanding of all or nothing thinking. I do not do this with a value assigned to abundance versus scarcity–just simply to make note of the client's experience. Abundance or scarcity can be measured in material possessions, the availability of love and affection versus neglect, or compromised access to caregivers. Abundance or scarcity can be measured in the amount of dialogue that occurred around difficult subjects versus the possible silence that pervades taboo subjects. Whatever the case may be, there are themes of abundance and scarcity that make themselves known throughout our lives. There is something about our early relationships with these "amounts" that sets the stage for our understanding of what is available to us in the present. Noting the formative power of this continuum greatly aids in our ability to non-pathologically make sense of our clients' functioning while still understanding the significance of their psychological experience of these themes.

Integration Versus Disintegration

Finally, I attempt to assess clients through the lens of integration versus disintegration. I maintain a keen eye on how integrated the important parts of one's identity are into their overall understanding of themselves. I also measure this integration against the pieces of their narrative that feel traumatic or if their stories are more predominantly authored by voices other than their own. In other words, are others' perceptions more integrated into their sense of self than their own? Or are traumatizing life experiences more powerfully felt than other powerful and essential pieces of the self? This is, of course, one way of reconceptualizing some of the self psychology ideas mentioned in Chapter 6. However, it can be broadly applied to all assessment.

Social work certainly subscribes to the notion that the authentic integration of pieces of our identity that are salient and bring us pride brings us closer to wellness. Social work also asserts that overintegration of traumatic pieces of our past moves us away from wellness. Tenuously, though, so does the disintegration of those pieces.

Simply put, we are interested in integration versus disintegration of volumes of material about our clients' lives. Positioning our understanding of psychological functioning along the lines of this continuum aids us in moving our work forward with clear direction and purpose.

Part 3

Practical
Considerations

Chapter 9
The Settings

When searching for social work employment, there are a few central questions to keep in mind. Of course, there is the salary, the overall vibe of the agency or setting, and the urgency with which you need a job. Aside from all of those stark realities, though, several questions are worth noting.

In this chapter, I will list a few of the possible settings in which you might find yourself during the early, middle, or even late stages of your career. It is not a comprehensive list, because there are so many possibilities that it would be impossible to list them all.

Much has already been written on the character of these settings, and I don't want to be repetitive. Instead, I want to speak from my experience of having visited hundreds of students in the field to give you a sense of what makes each of these settings clinical, whether the work you do there will be long- or short-term, whether supervision is typically included, what the bottom line treatment goals are, what the dominant treatment modalities are, and which theoretical orientations are most commonly employed.

Work With Children in Early Intervention Programs

How is it clinical? Work with children in early intervention or therapeutic settings often requires visits in the children's homes. This very fact renders the work extremely clinical, in that someone's home is just about the most vulnerable setting in which social work can take place. Even if the work doesn't feel clinical, the skills it takes to make a child or family feel respected in their own home is all clinical and extremely savvy. Further, bridging a connection when visiting children at home or in whatever setting they might be in (their school, possibly) requires a tremendous amount, again, of clinical savvy. There is a lot of work to negotiating systems in order to cultivate alliances in work with children. Once the alliance is formed, the sustenance of it is completely clinical and based on high attunement to attachment issues, understanding of complex developmental struggles, and building a type of trust for the child that may not exist anywhere else in the child's life.

Is it short- or long-term? It can certainly be both. Work with children, unlike many other forms of social work at this time, is often far more long-term. It sometimes lasts for several years.

Is there supervision? Almost all work with children requires a solid supervision structure. Because of the high stakes nature of this work and the extreme vulnerability of children, highly organized supervision by an accessible and experienced supervisor is going to be of tremendous support to you and would be ideal for this setting.

Bottom line treatment goals: Goals include the safety of the child, achieving developmental milestones, supporting the achievement of secure attachment, assessing for problematic behaviors, creating social support systems, and consistent success in academic settings.

Dominant treatment modalities: Family and individual. The individual work will likely require some training in play therapy.

Theoretical orientations commonly employed: Play therapy, systems theory, attachment theory, family systems theory, developmental psychology, and strengths based perspectives.

Human Services Agencies/Child Protective Services

How is it clinical? Work with human services agencies, otherwise known as children's services agencies, requires accurate and speedy assessment, engagement with defensive families who likely feel intruded upon by your presence, and very complex negotiations with multiple systems that will all require some sort of clinical acuity in order for solid relationships to be maintained.

Is it short- or long-term? It varies tremendously.

Is there supervision? Yes, there is always supervision for individuals operating without the highest level of licensure. However, because these agencies are government-run and the caseloads are high, it is very difficult to get a high level of attention, because resources are often scant.

Bottom line treatment goals: Determining the safety of a child, the safety of a home, the necessity of a foster care placement, making the foster care placement as seamless as possible, and fighting for family unification while simultaneously working toward individual child needs when family unification is too dangerous.

Dominant treatment modalities: Case management, assessment, referral making.

Theoretical orientations commonly employed: Family systems, systems theory, and strengths perspective.

Schools

How is it clinical? This work is often straight up clinical work, meeting with students who are either in crisis or simply struggling on a regular basis. Meetings with students last from 30-50 minutes and can happen once or twice a week. This is essentially not very different from traditional psychotherapy. However, the depth of the work might be different, because students do need to return to class intact. Further, some students also have an outside therapist whose goals you might need to be actively supporting or working with in tandem. Many don't, though, and the main source for clinical support that they are receiving is through the school. School social work can cover trauma, eating disorders, learning disorders, abuse, depression, anxiety, suicidality, and social struggles. There is no domain that school social work does not address, clinically.

Is it short- or long-term? It is often both, but given that treatment is not regulated by insurance, the freedom to work on a long-term basis is very available and liberating in this setting.

Is there supervision? It is certainly not guaranteed. Many schools do not have enough social workers to guarantee the provision of supervision, and securing supervision with someone who knows the school system well is ideal.

Bottom line treatment goals: To keep a child comfortably and non-disruptively in school, or to help determine that school is not an adequate setting at this time for the student. The bottom line is that treatment is all related to school, and the smooth functioning of the academic institution overall. This can sometimes have a negative impact on an individual treatment or child.

Dominant treatment modalities: Crisis response, de-escalation, individual, group, family, and psychoeducation.

Theoretical orientations commonly employed: A significant amount of behavioral modification, CBT, and trauma-informed CBT. Some smaller schools employ psychodynamic theories, but this is not generally the case.

Crisis Response Units

How is it clinical? Crisis response units are typically called into the homes of individuals who feel that they are in the midst of a mental health crisis. This work requires immediate assessment, alliance building, quick engagement capacity, and the ability to peacefully de-escalate. This requires a very specific set of clinical skills that are highly refined and take time to cultivate effectively.

Is it short- or long-term? Always short-term.

Is there supervision? The possibility for long-term supervision is very unlikely, but would be of tremendous import, particularly for the purpose of debriefing and de-escalating after intense clinical confrontations and crises. Finding ways of securing the opportunity to debrief in this setting will help to manage some of the deeper psychological impacts of working in this setting.

Bottom line treatment goals: Hospitalization or stabilization, de-escalation, astute assessment, quick decision-making, and making proper referrals.

Dominant treatment modalities: Assessment and de-escalation.

Theoretical orientations commonly employed: Strengths perspective, critical incident stress management skills, some CBT.

Partial Day Treatment

How is it clinical? Partial day treatment is clinical work, all day long. Partial day treatment programs can exist in either a hospital or an agency setting. They are sometimes considered to be step down programs, meaning a step down from inpatient and a step into traditional socialization.

Partial day treatment programs are designed to sustain individuals who are not quite unstable enough for inpatient treatment, but are functioning at a level that makes daily socialization or functionality challenging. The programs are highly reliant on a group format and often include groups, ranging from psychoeducation to process groups. Although individual work is done, it is not the focus of a partial day treatment program. The central goal is to increase toleration for socialization. Partial day treatment programs are designed to serve clients who fall on any spot along the diagnostic continuum.

A tremendous amount of time is spent with clients, and as a result, the clinical relationships that are formed can often become very deep and complex. Given the intimacy of the setting, nearly every aspect of a client's story is told, and many aspects of their functioning become unmasked.

Is it short- or long-term? It depends. Some partial day treatment programs have clients who are there for one to two weeks. Others have clients for as long as two years.

Is there supervision? There is almost always a hierarchy of mental health professionals in place in a partial day treatment program. This does not guarantee the provision of a well-established supervision program, but it does at least offer the possibility of colleagues with whom you can debrief and brainstorm.

Bottom line treatment goals: To aid in the transition back to daily functioning, the establishment or re-establishment of social networks, the creation and sustenance of self-esteem and self reflection, maintenance of symptoms of mental health disorders, stabilization of impulse control, anger management, possible procurement of employment, and secure reality testing.

Dominant treatment modalities: Most work in partial day treatment programs takes the form of group therapy. There is some case management and minimal individual treatment.

Theoretical orientations commonly employed: A tremendous amount of CBT is used, psychoeducation, strengths perspective, and some psychodynamic theory.

Community Mental Health

How is it clinical? Community mental health centers offer the opportunity to provide mental health counseling or psychotherapy to socioeconomically disenfranchised populations. The work is all clinical. The sessions usually last 45-50 minutes, and the depth of the work can become high. This work also requires one to work along the diagnostic continuum.

Is it short- or long-term? Depending upon the limitations of insurance coverage, the work can be long- or short-term. Given that most community mental health agencies are committed to providing treatment to uninsured populations, the work can frequently become very long-term.

Is there supervision? It is not guaranteed. Again, this is because caseloads are high and resources are low. Many clinicians working in community mental health agencies seek outside supervision, which can be very difficult because communicating the nuances of each community mental health agency structure is not a simple task. Adequate time to discuss the bureaucratic functioning will promote the success of supervision for workers in this type of setting.

Bottom line treatment goals: Symptom management, the establishment of long-term healthy relational functioning, and whatever goal the client states, which is a wonderful way to work.

Dominant treatment modalities: Mainly individual, but can include couples, family, and group.

Theoretical orientations commonly employed: This often varies from agency to agency, and often from clinician to clinician. There is a lot of freedom and variability in this way.

Domestic Violence

How is it clinical? This work is clinical in the effort it takes to work with survivors to understand the cycles of power and control, to recognize the very complex nature of repetition compulsion, and to work almost exclusively in the constant assessment of the stages of change. Further, domestic violence work is trauma work that requires an astute understanding of the intricate impact that trauma has upon the mind.

Is it short- or long-term? The work can take place in shelters or assistance programs, so the types of opportunities are varied. For the most part, the work is short-term, rarely lasting more than six months to a year.

Is there supervision? Yes, ideally. Because of the high stakes nature of the work and high level of fatality associated with it, there is a very well established network of supervision typically in place in domestic violence settings. There are certainly agencies that simply don't have the resources for this. Because of the high likelihood for vicarious traumatization in this type of setting, advocating for some type of supervision will create a more sustainable experience in this specific setting.

Bottom line treatment goals: To keep survivors and their children safe and alive.

Dominant treatment modalities: Psychoeducation, case management, individual work, and support/group work.

Theoretical orientations commonly employed: Feminist theories, psychoeducation, systems theory, strengths perspectives, CBT, psychodynamic theories, and motivational interviewing.

Rape Crisis Centers

How is it clinical? This work is designed to re-create the possibility of trust and a sense of safety in clients who have been violated and lost those essential states of mind. Given that this work rests completely on the creation of a sound therapeutic alliance, it is entirely clinical work.

Is it short- or long-term? It is typically more short-term than long, but there are exceptions to this rule.

Is there supervision? I have seen this vary quite a bit from agency to agency and cannot say that there is a consistent theme in terms of supervision in rape crisis centers. Some offer tremendous supervision. Others do not seem to have that structure in place.

Bottom line treatment goals: The reduction of PTSD symptoms, the re-establishment of trusting relationships, the reduction in self-injurious behaviors or other sequelae that result after sexual assault, the re-establishment of self-esteem, and moves toward future safety planning.

Dominant treatment modalities: Individual and group treatment.

Theoretical orientations commonly employed: Feminist theories, narrative therapies, strengths-based approaches, psychodynamic theories, and trauma focused therapies.

Medical Setting/ICU/ER/Pediatric or Adult

How is it clinical? Although not always clearly clinical, working with families in a medical setting requires a tremendous amount of clinical engagement at an acutely vulnerable time. This is a time when families have to make complicated and terrifying decisions. They feel inept at navigating labyrinth-like bureaucratic structures, and they are dealing with medical issues that feel completely overwhelming. A social worker is a bridge that translates between one world (the medical one) and another (the pedestrian one) at a time when translation is of the utmost import. The work is fast-paced and requires a good amount of calm in the face of chaos, a complicated and valued clinical skill.

There are also hospital social work positions that provide the opportunity to work in a more long-term manner, providing psychotherapy. These might include working with oncology, chronic illness, or rehabilitation patients. There is no real way to generalize social work in a medical setting because of the highly varied manner in which social workers can be used.

Is it short- or long-term? This is highly dependent on the unit of the hospital, the needs of the patients, and the duration of the stay.

Is there supervision? Because hospitals are well-established networks, the availability of supervision is probable, but not guaranteed. Social work departments are staffed at many levels, and there is significant room for support, supervision, and collaboration. There is also the opportunity for inter-disciplinary support that is rare and exciting. Given the number of stressors and whether or not the hospital is a teaching hospital, the possibility for consistent supervision is highly variable.

Bottom line treatment goals: To help patients and families make wise and prudent treatment decisions while supporting them on a spiritual, emotional, psychological, and social level. The goals also require us to set up adequate discharge plans and to offer solace during times of intense grief and pain.

Dominant treatment modalities: Case management, discharge planning, family meetings.

Theoretical orientations commonly employed: Psychoeducation and systems theory.

Substance Use Disorders

How is it clinical? Substance use disorder treatment can take place in an inpatient, outpatient, or partial day treatment setting. All of these settings require the use of refined clinical skills to work with clients to stop using drugs and/or alcohol. This requires an in-depth knowledge of the impact of trauma on the mind, the role of socioeconomics in substance use disorders, the stages of change, addiction and all of its permutations, and the impact that addiction has on family and relationships.

Is it short- or long-term? The work is often short-term because of the structure of many of the settings where it takes place. However, there are opportunities for more long-term work in settings such as methadone clinics or other outpatient settings that work specifically with drugs and alcohol.

Is there supervision? Yes, there is often supervision in these settings. But, again, this is not guaranteed. Finding a supervisor well versed in current substance use disorder research and thinking will be crucial because of the highly specialized nature of this sub-field.

Bottom line treatment goals: Depending on the setting, the goal is either harm reduction or abstinence. This distinction will have a large impact on the work that is done. In either case, the underlying treatment goal is to reduce the impact of drugs and alcohol on someone's life while restoring or creating healthier aspects of daily living.

Dominant treatment modalities: Group, individual, couples, family, and 12-step meetings.

Theoretical orientations commonly employed: The 12-step principles, CBT, psychodynamic work, trauma theory, and motivational interviewing.

Inpatient Mental Health

How is it clinical? Working with clients at the height of acuity of their mental health struggles is intense and nuanced work. Clients are typically treated in an inpatient setting when their symptoms are producing psychotic features, such as auditory or visual hallucinations. Clients can also be inpatients if they are at risk of hurting themselves or others. In many ways, working with clients in an inpatient setting is working with them at their psychological "low." Clinically, for some, this is a privilege. It is a raw space for many, and accompanying clients at this point in their journey toward wellness requires a huge amount of tolerance for extreme affect, low amounts of impulse control and reality testing, and sometimes minimal insight.

Is it short- or long-term? The work is nearly uniformly short-term, given today's insurance environment. Long-term stays in inpatient psychiatric settings rarely, if ever, are covered. There are some options for long-term inpatient work, but this is usually covered by the family or the patient's own private pay.

Is there supervision? Typically, yes, supervision is a well-established aspect of inpatient work. However, inpatient mental health settings often subscribe to a highly medicalized model of thinking. This can limit the ways in which one can perform and explore one's social work identity. Given this limitation, having an outside supervisor with a solid grasp of social work values can deeply enhance one's experience of working in an inpatient setting.

Bottom line treatment goals: Stabilization, symptom reduction, solid referral sources, and discharge.

Dominant treatment modalities: Mainly group, often family, with minimal individual interaction.

Theoretical orientations commonly employed: Psychoeducation, often CBT, rarely psychodynamic.

Geriatric Settings

How is it clinical? This work can take place in a senior citizens center in the community or a nursing home. It can also take place in the homes of aging adults through case management or services for the aging, in retirement communities, or in areas of a hospital. Offering people support toward the end of their life and enhancing this phase of their life can offer considerable fulfillment. It is also a highly clinical achievement, given how underserved and under-engaged this population is. The amount of clinical reward associated with this work is often unreported, but I have seen social workers grow clinically working in this particular realm of our field, because of the complex histories of the clients, the wisdom of the clients, and how much there is to learn from this population.

Is it short- or long-term? Long-term.

Is there supervision? Yes, frequently. However, there is a good amount of bereavement that comes with working in a geriatric setting, and agencies are not always adept at addressing the grief of the work. Outside supervision can help someone address the loss that comes with being in a geriatric setting, and processing this is of terrific import.

Bottom line treatment goals: Establishing a decent quality of life, cultivating social stimulation, maintaining family support, managing health issues and medical relationships.

Dominant treatment modalities: There is a large amount of variation.

Theoretical orientations commonly employed: Largely strengths based, with psychoeducation.

Hospice

How is it clinical? Some cannot imagine working in hospice. Those who work in hospice cannot imagine anything else. It is said that the intimacy that comes with this work is simply incomparable. The work is raw, vulnerable, and simply clinical. It requires aiding families to say what feels unsayable before having to say good-bye. It also requires families to say good-bye when they feel they can't.

A good amount of the work requires a facing up to denial, an understanding of illness, an explanation of the dying process, and an encouragement of tolerating affect and emotion that feels intolerable in order to pave the way for healthy grieving processes.

Is it short- or long-term? By definition, hospice services are provided for six months or less. There are rare exceptions when the patient is in hospice care for longer than this. Also, longer-term relationships with the bereaved can be formed through the provision of support services after the patient's death.

Is there supervision? Generally, yes. There is often a good amount of burnout that comes with this work that is best supported by additional, outside supervision, from a supervisor who is not similarly burned out by the shared experiences in the work.

Bottom line treatment goals: Easing the individual and the family through the death and dying process, hoping to aid in the maintenance of as much psychological integrity as possible. The work also includes extending support services to grieving family members during the bereavement period.

Dominant treatment modalities: This is largely free-flowing, often in home, and unstructured. The modalities are informed by whatever is called for in the moment.

Theoretical orientations commonly employed: Psychoeducation, family systems and strengths perspective, stages of change, and motivational interviewing.

Private Psychotherapy Practice

How is it clinical? This work is completely clinical and highly complicated to enter. First, working privately automatically introduces a high level of self disclosure. Everything from the address of your building or office to the furnishings becomes grist for the therapeutic mill. A lot becomes known about the social worker in private practice before any interpersonal exchanges have even occurred. Secondly, most of the financial interactions between clients and social workers (which we are largely protected from in agencies) become clinical issues. Everything from the fee to late cancellations becomes fodder for complicating the treatment—albeit complicating it in a very important and nuanced manner. When the social worker is out sick, this becomes a clinical issue, as do snow days. Private practice largely catapults into a realm of intense clinical meaning making, in which every layer of our interactions holds deep psychological significance and warrants exploration. Although this is largely true in agencies, as well, often the agency structure does something to legislate a good amount of how interactions unfold between the client and clinician.

Is it short- or long-term? The answer depends on whether or not you choose to take insurance. Many insurers will only cover a finite number of sessions, rendering the work short term. However, there are often financial arrangements that can be made with clients that allow the treatment to continue. The decision about whether or not to take insurance is almost as big as the decision to go into private practice at all. Without insurance, many practitioners create their own sliding scales and find a way to openly discuss financial limitations and needs with their clients. In many ways, taking insurance keeps us out of these complicated dialogues, but it leaves the treatment highly vulnerable to bureaucratic systems that largely survey how the treatment is unfolding.

Is there supervision? If you pay for it, yes. Supervision for private practice is of terrific import, given how lonely the work of private practice can feel. Supervision often ameliorates intense feelings of isolation and keeps practitioners from becoming overly reliant on their own judgment.

Bottom line treatment goals: This varies from practice to practice and from client to client. Part of the luxury of working in a private practice is that treatment goals can be incredibly flexible. Further, if a treatment goal is achieved, this does not put the treatment in jeopardy. Oftentimes, working in a setting that is closely beholden to treatment goals makes the reaching of these goals a very mixed experience. The goal has been reached, but this might signify the severing of a therapeutic attachment. Private practice often allows clients to reach their goals and to comfortably create new ones.

Dominant treatment modalities: You can easily perform family therapy, couples therapy, group therapy, or individual therapy in your own private practice. Of course, space is an issue when running groups, but there are typically spaces that can be easily rented to support any group.

Theoretical orientations commonly employed: This is totally up to you. As a private practitioner, you are free to employ whatever orientation feels the most right for you.

These are just a few of the settings where social workers are employed. There are too many to count. Our field is almost uniquely characterized by its simultaneous diversity and unity. This is a sketch of how to evaluate some of the settings. It is important to assess for yourself what makes your work clinical, how important it is to you to work on a short- or long-term basis, what modality is most comfortable to you, and what theoretical orientations you are most eager to learn more about or practice. This guide is designed to help you begin to create your own assessment of settings you are considering, so you can select your own employment setting in the most informed way possible, with eyes open and clear decisions made.

Chapter 10
Money, Money, Money

"We all imagine that others are really organized and together with their money. Most people are not." Susan Kennedy, 2002

If theory is the proverbial hat that we wear on our clinical heads, then finances are certainly the shoes on our feet. To find clinical success, a certain internal peace must be made with ourselves as worthy of a livable salary. This process, for social workers, is made thorny by our awareness of socioeconomic and racial inequity. Seeing the suffering of our clients makes determining our own financial self-worth an often guilt-ridden and thought-provoking journey, if we are willing to let ourselves be open to the journey at all. It is difficult to remain conscious about it. There is a significant amount of silence around money in social work. It almost feels like a scheme to keep us quiet about our often paltry salaries. I am hoping that this chapter serves to deconstruct some of the powerful shame that we can feel about needing money as professional adults who work hard, are often raising families, and deserve to live lives that feel adequately comfortable. This is a level of entitlement that, unfortunately, often eludes social workers. As experts in human rights, social workers often remain ignorant to their own human rights. Living a financially stable life is a human rights issue.

Of the 100 social workers who were interviewed for this book, 31% articulated a sense of financial security. Thirty percent stated that they sometimes feel financially secure, and 40% do not. This is both scary and sad. These numbers can be understood as a by-product of our underpayment, which is certainly a pervasive issue. I believe they might also be understood as a by-product of our collective lack of feelings of self worth, a highly related and also pervasive issue. Chicken or egg, poor salary offerings or poor sense of professional self worth, financial issues facing social workers are substantial, steep, and worthy of serious dialogue. This is a dialogue that needs to happen internally in the mind of each individual social worker, as well as within social work communities, to bring the shame of the need for money, the sense of not having enough, and the wish for more out of hiding.

More importantly, though, it is imperative for us to have the psychological availability to be able to do our work well. This work requires a lot of us–a lot of psychic and emotional space. When our minds are crowded with feelings of worry, anxiety, and fear, it is nearly impossible to give our clients what they need. Facing our money issues is a journey for ourselves, but it is also a clearing for our clients, making us truly available to them as excellent social workers.

Facts, Not Feelings

I have a good number of social workers as clients, both as clinical patients and as supervisees. The dialogue about fees with this particular population is always a compelling one. With lawyers, doctors, or nurses, the discussion about fees is often more straightforward. I don't want to oversimplify this. The discussion about fees is always complicated. However, with social workers, the dialogue has a unique texture. Social workers often want to pay more than they have, often feel that they owe me what they feel I am "worth," and will often stretch themselves to make payments that make the treatment or the supervision very difficult to sustain. It is hard, payments between social workers. This is essentially a very complex communication–one social worker to another about worth, my worth versus yours, yours versus mine. I will often ask my social worker clients to go back before agreeing to a fee and to figure out their budgets.

Budgeting is hard for anyone. There is no question about that. Few people know the stark reality of the numbers. There is something particularly fuzzy about this for social workers, though. My hypothesis about this is that social workers feel stuck in some sort of purgatory or netherworld. Social workers are well aware of the poverty and oppression of their clients. This makes it problematic to not feel some sort of privilege when simply earning a paycheck every two weeks, when having a roof and sustenance. These "privileges" keep us looking away from how we are suffering. They keep us looking away from what we actually need and what we don't have and how we are often dangerously stretching. We are afraid of our privilege, and we are afraid of our scarcity, in equal parts. And we are often stuck because of it. This is, of course, a macro take on it. There are then the individual intrapsychic issues that brought each of us into the field and play out on a financial level that also need to be addressed.

The amount of money that each of us needs is essentially a black and white number based on our living expenses, our student loans, and our family obligations. I say this because, upon graduation, the salary ranges that you will be offered are huge. You can easily be offered $18,000 or $23,000 or $42,000. The range is large and highly dependent on varying agency resources. And you will get anxious and want to take a salary that is below what you can live on.

Part of how you will take a salary that is below what you can live on is twofold. First, you can't wait for a higher salary, and that is completely legitimate. Second, you have not been completely honest with yourself about how much you need to earn, because on some level you are too ashamed of it, don't think that you are worth it, or don't think you can find a job that will pay it. This is the type of thinking, based in deep feelings of scarcity, that keeps us so entrenched in salaries that leave us feeling undervalued. This type of thinking is based on dishonesty with ourselves about what we actually need in order to live in a way that feels okay.

What Is Your Number?

I often ask students to try to come up with their "number" (bottom line salary), whatever their number is. This number is very different depending on whether or not their student loans are public or private (meaning that they can be adjusted for income-based repayment plans). This number is also very different depending on whether or not a job is offering supervision. If a job is offering supervision, this goes a long way toward financially helping to get you to the next level of licensure. If you are responsible for paying for outside supervision, you can calculate that as an extra expense, thereby rendering your "number" (what you need to earn) higher.

To come up with your number, you need to calculate your own expenses and do a lot of talking to others about what their starting salaries were. Even though your expectation needs to reflect the reality of what you need, it also needs to reflect the reality of what you can make. The only way to learn about this is to start practicing talking about it. The more taboo you feel the dialogue around salary is, the more disabled you are going to feel in this process.

Below is a chart of the salary ranges of 100 social workers (as of early 2014) who have been in the field for a range of years, so it certainly does not indicate solely starting salaries. The range of time in the field for these respondents is zero to 35 years. These social workers are also largely based in Pennsylvania, which has two large urban areas skewing the salary ranges slightly higher than non-urban areas. All of that said, the notion of being paid less than $30,000 is substandard for our field and should be considered as such.

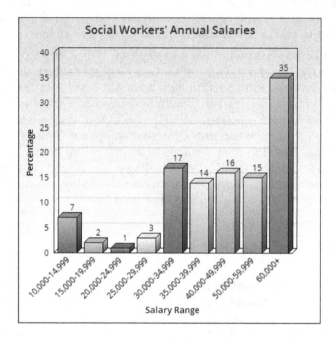

My Story

When I graduated with my MSW in 2005, the number in my head was $50,000. This was a number that was completely based on a feeling; it had no objective standing at all. I felt that I had gone to graduate school and should earn $50,000. I had had a lot of jobs before school, ranging in salary from $36,000 (in a nonprofit) to $52,000 (at a financial services firm), and I didn't want to earn less by entering the field. I had no idea what $50,000 really meant in the field, what it would exclude me from, and what jobs it would even allow me to consider. I also had no idea what it would look like on a monthly basis. A salary is such a theoretical number in a lot of ways. How it plays out on a monthly basis is a different story entirely.

I had around $85,000 in student loan debt at the time. I didn't know which loans were federal or private. I had no idea what that would mean per month. I just said to myself, *I have almost 85k in student loan debt, so I need to make 50k.* As you may or may not know, you don't have to start paying your loans until six months after you graduate, so I considered that period a grace period for panicking around my job search.

I immediately started fee-for-service work at the agency where I had interned during my final year of school. Fee-for-service work is available if you want it. There is nothing particularly wrong with it, but it carries with it significant complications if you are relying on it as your sole source of income. There is rarely health insurance with fee-for-service work, and supervision is rarely included. (You typically have to pay for it out of pocket.) If your client doesn't come, you don't get paid. I would say that this is fairly thorny territory for a novice clinician. Relying on your client's attendance for your income does not make it easy to build healthy clinical relationships. Further, having so little income that you can't afford to be supervised on these very fragile clinical relationships further endangers how soundly you can practice. Every time I had a no show, I would panic. I felt there was no one with whom I could have a productive conversation about this, frequently using my partner as my supervisor.

During this time, I was interviewing for perfectly reasonable jobs with salaries of around $32,000-36,000 and was ceremoniously turning them down. There is one in particular that I still think back on with regret, because I think I would have loved it. It was working with women veterans in a transitional housing complex. I finally started to realize that I needed to relax my standards and take a job for $40,000, and that I could use the fee-for-service work to augment my salary.

So, my first social work position was at a college counseling center making $42,000 (before taxes) a year. What this meant per month (after taxes) in take-home pay was $2,632.45. I urge all of you to use a salary calculator for your state to determine what an annual salary means for your monthly life. The most reliable one I have found is *http://www.adp.com*. This job provided supervision, which essentially meant that my salary was also paying for my next level of licensure. I also received $1,000 a year toward continuing education credits needed to maintain licensure, a tax deduction for the University (and for any agency). The fact is that the salary was great for a starting social worker. Living on $2,632 a month is not easy, though, when you are in an urban area with a lot of student loan debt. This is why you need to also know the structure of how you will get raises and if there are ways to augment your salary.

There is a lot in this story. First, there is flexibility and inflexibility, and I believe that both are important here. My standard shifted, but not to the point at which it became sacrificial. Second, the university where I was employed offered me several ways in which it was willing to invest in me. I sincerely believe that if the salary is not what you would like it to be, there are several ways that agencies can make up for this with vacation time, investments in your learning, and opportunities for rich supervision. I think social work jobs, even your first one, can be structured as mutual investments—them in you and you in them. This is not like starting to work at a law firm, where the clear return on investment for you is a huge salary and for them is indentured servitude. Ideally, you are joining an agency or an organization that you believe in and whose values you want to promote. You are also growing and learning and worthy of their investment in you. Your agency knows this.

Salary and Sustainability

You are not a seasoned social worker and can't be hired as such. A bit of education should be part of your benefits package. I think it is fair to expect this. Everyone knows that two years of graduate school training is quite short and that it is only the beginning of your refinement professionally. Although you will have a huge amount of responsibility in your first job, this doesn't mean that a deepening of expertise cannot be a reasonable and formalized part of the proposition. It is also fair to want complete transparency around how your salary will look year to year, so you know exactly how sustainable the situation is.

When answering the question of sustainability, you must ask yourself several questions about your own life. I don't know all of them, but I have a few ideas that I will list here that might help get you thinking:

- How do you determine your standard of living?
- Are roommates okay or do you need to live alone?
- Can you handle a studio?
- Do you have flexibility on neighborhoods?
- Can you live without a car? Can you live with a car?
- Do you know how much monthly public transportation costs where you live, and does it outweigh the cost of a car?

- Do you want to be in therapy? Are you comfortable with someone who will provide sliding scale, or would you prefer a wider array of choices?

- Can you live without health insurance? Or are you willing to pay for your own if your employer doesn't provide it?

- Can you live with health insurance that does not provide mental health coverage, or is that unacceptable to you?

- Do you need to be a member of a gym?

- If you are a parent, are you comfortable with the local public schools, or are you considering private school?

- Are you comfortable with the possibility of your child needing to take out student loans in the future, or would you prefer to have a clear college savings plan in mind?

- Do you want to own a home one day?

- Do you want to be in the position of furthering your training (i.e., more education) without taking on significantly more debt?

- Do you have outside support, and are you willing/comfortable taking it?

- For how long are you comfortable taking it, if necessary?

- How much are you willing to live with and without? This question includes ideas about where you shop for food, where you dine out, a recreational budget, vacation, and so on.

- Do you need savings?

- Are you comfortable living paycheck to paycheck?

- What past variables are affecting your thinking about these issues?

- What are your main obstacles to achieving financial fulfillment?

Student Loans

First and foremost, I want to acknowledge that the student loan situation is a complete and total morass for most of us. We often feel that the person to our right and to our left has it figured out. No one has it figured out. No one. The student loan companies are completely banking on us remaining unconscious around our student loans and are confident in our continued complacency.

This isn't just true for social workers, but I do think that social workers do feel particularly disempowered when dealing with student loan debt. I am not completely sure what this is about. I do wonder if advocating for our clients all day leaves us partly inept at advocating for ourselves, at even seeing ourselves as individuals who deserve our own self-advocacy. Whatever the underlying causation, it is critical to address the student loan repayment process. Without intense diligence, managing student loans is overwhelming at best and paralyzing at worst. Without a real feeling of financial empowerment, the paralysis often wins. Graduates and new clinicians need to figure out how much they owe each month, how much they can consolidate, and what repayment programs and options are available to them. Without this information, each of us enters the job search in a highly misinformed manner.

Determining the answers to these questions requires a certain level of entitlement to the answers. If you go to *http://www.finaid. org/calculators/icr.phtml* and enter the information that you have, it will help you to determine what your student loan payments will be each month. This calculator will help you determine how much you will need to pay and how much of it is flexible (federal) versus fixed (private).

It is hard to even know which company owns your debt. I believe it essential for us to maintain a spreadsheet (Excel works fine) of each of our student loans (most of us have many), the phone numbers of each student loan company, the interest rate of each loan, the repayment terms (how many months), and whether the loans do or do not offer an income-based repayment plan. The second you get a letter in the mail that says your loan has been sold (and this will happen often), the loan needs to be updated in your spreadsheet. I would also suggest that you check your credit report annually and match it against your spreadsheet to verify that the loan companies are supplying the right information to the credit agencies. Student loan mistakes make it harder to get a mortgage than almost anything else, and it is so easy to look the other way, given the labyrinth-like functioning of the entire industry.

I would argue that managing student loan debt feels almost like a second job at first. It does not always require a high level of vigilance, but initially it does. I think that taking a close look at things at least every six months is of tremendous import. Shying away from dealing with this will keep your life in a state of chaos that will make practicing good social work nearly impossible. In Chapter 12, I reference the complex socioeconomics of self-care dialogues. I truly believe this is where authentic self-care lies—looking at our financial realities in the face and dealing with them fearlessly.

Perhaps there is shame in having student loan debt at all. This is entirely possible. Many people are in hiding from the people they feel the closest to, around how much debt they have. There is a huge culture of privacy around these numbers that keeps us feeling very alone in our debt experiences. Even though the dialogue has become more normalized, I would argue that individual experiences with debt are still fairly hushed. There is a lot of paradox in this, for us as social workers. We fight very hard to end the shame associated with the socioeconomic struggles of our clients, hoping to bring the travesty of poverty out of hiding. When it comes to our own relationship with our own debt, we frequently fall silent.

Below is a chart that highlights the average amount that social workers in my survey are paying per month in student loan debt. The majority of us are paying around $550, suggesting that we each generally have around $75,000 in educational debt. Some of us have less, and many, many of us have more. I say this to try to normalize it and to begin to give voice to the reality of it. I also want to note that around 10% of us are paying almost $1,000 a month on student loan debt. With the salaries we are offered, this is a serious issue that must be addressed collectively as a profession.

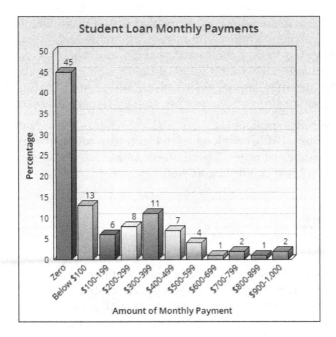

Investments

The fact is that to have a successful social work career, you are going to have to invest in your career to a varying degree, depending on what your goals are. If your wish is to remain in agency work, I would say that the investment is less than if you would like to have a private practice or if you would like to teach some day at a university. Either way, though, the need for investment is there. First, the licensing exam itself is an expense. Second, maintaining the license with continuing education credits (the number of hours required varies from state to state) is another expense. Investment is inevitable, so intending to do it wisely and mindfully is an excellent goal.

As a recent grad, you will be eligible for discounts on some professional investments. Most locales have a clinical social work society that is absolutely worth joining. These societies will often have an electronic mailing list that posts jobs, gives you access to supervisors who offer supervision at a reduced fee, alert you to book club meetings, and announce other continuing education opportunities in the area. If the average annual membership fee for an organization like this is $150, it might be as low as $30 for a recent graduate. Similar discounts can be applied to national organizations such as the National Association of Social Workers (NASW), which offers a transitional membership fee for those who joined as students. If you are interested in sampling what is out there, the time to do it is post graduation. Further, the investments you make in these organizations are fully or partially tax deductible, which is something in which you are going to want to become extremely interested.

Other investments that are worth considering for a new graduate are journal subscriptions, which can also be highly discounted for new social workers. There are conferences that will have discounted entry fees for you, as well.

Branding

The issue, of course, is: How do you choose what post graduate option would fulfill you the most and would also serve to promote the idiosyncratic way in which you plan to distinguish yourself from your colleagues? This is where the question of becoming savvy comes in. It is worth beginning to consider early on after graduation how you would like to *brand* yourself. All of these decisions can be made through this lens. Let's say you have an interest in GLBT issues or substance use disorders. These simple tenets can guide you in which journals you subscribe to, which conferences you want to attend, and which supervisors you become interested in talking to. This early branding is nowhere near a lifetime commitment, but it is a way of refining your investment to become more specifically aligned with possible long-term career goals. The reason I suggest this is that your first job will have a lot of goals for you, and it will become very hard to not become a mold for them to sculpt. To some extent, that will have to happen, but you are also in charge of your career and your future. Any investment you make, with YOUR money, should be in the brand of social worker that you want to become.

Each year past graduation, it makes sense to increase your budget for your brand. The first year, the investment will likely be in supervision and continuing education. The second year is the same. After two years, you will likely become more specific about your goals, possibly creating a website to augment what you are doing and offering possibilities for consulting, writing, or whatever feels most right at the time. You might start to consider making business cards for yourself. None of this means that you are starting a private practice; it means that you are developing an identity as a social worker in the community who might not be completely beholden to any one agency. It means that you are in charge of your career with a certain level of unabashedness.

There are ways in which this can go too far. Some social workers spend much of their time on Twitter and Facebook waiting for clients to come. There are other ways in which you can stay completely ensconced in a way that will keep you from finding like-minded social workers or clients that might lend tremendous meaning to your work.

Finding financial freedom as a social worker is the very painful reality of having to invest in one's career beyond the cost of tuition. After paying steep tuition for years, this can feel like a terrifying prospect, particularly when the return on investment feels completely elusive. I don't think it is wise to hand over too much money too quickly, and there is ample opportunity to do that. Wise, careful, and frugal investment can be done incrementally over time in a way that honors that financial moment that you are in while positioning for strong future possibilities.

We All Have a Money Story

Because you are a social worker now, you clearly know that we all have complex psychological histories. Embedded in this complex history is a money story that we carry with us. This money story informs nearly every financial decision we make, whether it is what salary we expect or what brand of toilet paper we buy. These decisions are entrenched and intergenerational. Our work is to release ourselves from the grips of these compelling narratives in order to gain access to our own financial voices, desires, and most importantly, our own financial needs. We all have the responsibility to ask ourselves: What is psychologically informing my financial functioning? And in this question is another question: How do I talk to myself about money?

For the most part, unfortunately, our financial narratives become self-fulfilling prophecies. I wouldn't say that this is entirely true in every field, but given that there are many social work jobs that don't pay adequately and it is easy to become over-used in this field, it is not difficult to fulfill prophecies that match stories of low self worth and shame.

I have rented five offices at this point in my short private practice career, and each one of them has told a story of a deep intrapsychic struggle I have had with what I deserve and how much space in the world I believe I am allowed to take up. The first two offices were one-day-a-week sublets of someone else's space, using someone else's furniture, and fitting into someone else's schedule. Of course, this was fitting for where I was in my career. It was also very fitting for where I was in my mind–afraid of making an investment in my career or in myself. This also meant that I was very comfortable taking highly reduced fees, making it nearly impossible to support myself or my family. When I finally was ready to move into my long-term office, I decided to take notes on the conversations I was having with my mother about furnishing the office. I took the notes to therapy, so I could get a sense of why I would become so terrified of purchasing a mere umbrella stand. I am so glad I did that, because I needed the information in black and white. Otherwise, it felt to me as normal as air; I just breathed it in and breathed it out.

I have a student who is three months into a 10-month placement, and they offered her a job there already. The job would only be 30% clinical, with the rest of her time spent on administrative tasks. She has zero interest in administrative work. She thinks she should take it. She wonders what I think. She thinks she should just say "yes." I think it is interesting that someone who has invested so much in her education and is only 60% through her education is already considering taking a job that does not support the reasons she entered school to begin with. It would be one thing if she had been on the job market for months, but she hasn't been on the job market at all.

The fact is that she is terrified. She is operating from a place of significant scarcity. And this is not unreal. This isn't just a fiction because of her psychological history. She will, in fact, be graduating with no support or help. It will be a free fall for her. It's good to get a job offer. But she is completely missing how empowered she is in the position. After such a short time there, she is clearly desired by the agency. She has demonstrated something to them that is clearly compelling. They are also stating, very overtly, that they are not interested in doing a candidate search.

My student always sits in the back row in class. She is extremely quiet. She submits her papers before anyone else. She is also amazingly smart, and she is theoretically sophisticated and astute. In this situation, she has all the power in the world. She feels none at all. She once referenced being a really good kid for her parents. I would argue that this theme has held true. And it is a dangerous one, for her. I think that she can easily ask for the job to be at least 50% clinical, if not more. She can also say that she is going to go on the job market and get back to them. The longer she is there, the more appealing to them she is going to become.

Her belief, though, is that the more they get to know her, the less they are going to want her. These deeply held beliefs about needing to be good, about ultimately being found out as undesirable, will render her underpaid and unsatisfied. Without interrogating the holding power of these voices, these stories, she is hostage to them and so is her career. As she tries to free her clients from similar fates, it is her responsibility to begin to do the same for herself and, in many ways, this work begins with salary negotiations and job searches.

Our money stories have deep roots, which cannot simply be undone and are not necessarily always bad. It isn't that simple. We cannot shed our histories, and that isn't exactly the goal. Instead, we need to become sharply aware of how our story is scripting our expectations for what we deserve in the field, financially.

The field of social work is a complicated one, financially. There is a lot of opportunity for exploitation. Hierarchically, it often feels as if we are at the bottom of the totem pole in relation to our colleagues with similar degrees. Our journey toward respect, equality, and fair financial remuneration is one that we must move toward with vigilance. This is a vigilance that can only be cultivated through a careful self-study of what we want to take with us from our pasts and what we want to leave behind. This might include role models who were highly disciplined, had amazing work ethics, lived within their means, spoke honestly about their debts, and made strong short-

and long-term financial decisions. Or we might want to shed feelings of scarcity, panic, chaos, a tendency to hide, to be overly compliant, legacies of underachievement or compulsive overachievement, and uneven work/life balances.

Some might say that graduation simply leads to a job search, and on many levels, it does. But for social workers, we are becoming models for our clients, idealized objects. We will certainly be overly idealized, and we are going to be completely imperfect–proudly so, I hope. That said, we have a responsibility, given the gravity of our role in our clients' lives, to remain conscious in our own, and to keep "our side of the street clean." To enter our careers in a way that is highly untethered is a part of honoring this commitment.

Our True Work

One of the strengths and weaknesses of the field of social work, as I have mentioned, is that there are many ways to make money and not a lot of ways to make a lot of money. Social workers have the possibility to work all the time, to work a lot of different jobs, and to still not quite make ends meet. The more jobs that social workers perform, the more suffering they can become exposed to, making the guilt about their own struggle even more uncomfortable and complicated to face. Let me be clear in stating that guilt, very plainly, is an unproductive emotion. Our work, as social workers, is to discover our *true work*, and guilt will certainly obscure our ability to secure that knowledge. Many people work at jobs that drain or frustrate them, stay in these roles because of guilt, and then feel that there is literally no energy left to search for what feels more or most right.

This is a field that truly affords us the opportunity for rich, constant, and textured fulfillment. I mean that. I wake up and come home every day somehow stimulated by my work. I find many supervisees who feel the same way. I also have supervisees with caseloads of 80-100 clients, with more paperwork than they can possibly manage, who feel that they cannot think straight. These supervisees are often underpaid and are also working a second job at a restaurant or a coffee shop to stay afloat. They have counterparts in supervision group without any more experience making $10,000 more with a caseload of 13. The variation is simply astounding.

Somehow, the agencies that don't pay adequately keep getting staffed, despite high turnover, so the sustainability is there for the agency itself. All I can say is that it feels essential to guard against burnout early in your career, and to expose yourself to other possibilities through group supervision, networking, fee-for-service opportunities, or per diem hours in a hospital. Anything that gives you the sense of possibility is worth considering.

I have a supervisee who feels completely misaligned with the values of a charter school where she works, but the salary is great. She recently started doing fee-for-service work with adolescent girls in recovery. She is there four hours a week. These four hours are her *true work* hours. This is where she is most alive and most engaged. The work at the charter school makes this possible, deepening the meaning of the charter school position in many ways.

I have another supervisee who is currently working as a case manager for Holocaust survivors. There is a tremendous amount of stress associated with the work, particularly in relationship to managing the younger generations of survivors. She feels that there is a huge amount of demand put upon her–that she is essentially asked to do impossible tasks on a daily basis. The flip side is, though, that she believes that she is ushering out a dying breed of bold survivors with whom she will never have the opportunity to work again. And she won't. This is her *true work*. Amidst a lot of daily struggle, frustration, and a sense of impotence is a commitment to daily meaning in what she is doing.

The search for and ultimate identification of this takes quite a bit of time, and I would argue that there is no rush. I would also argue that it is completely okay if your *true work* does not take up the majority of your hours, because the level of reward associated with it is so sustaining.

In my work, I have spent half of my time teaching and half my time practicing. I also do quite a bit of thesis advising, supervising, and public speaking. I cannot say that any one of these feels most "true." What I do know is that social work has provided me with a lot of ways to make money, and that being a social worker makes it very hard to ever say no. It is an inherent occupational hazard. I also know that these roles complement each other because of the way our field works. It all comes together somehow, because of the shared values of our work–because of the unique shared culture of how we think. There is equal opportunity for diversification and exhaustion, and we need to be open to and guarded against both of these realities, in search of our true work and in protection of our personal selves.

Part 4

Practice Matters

Chapter 11
Making Use of Supervision

My experience in supervision, as a supervisee, has been both complex and varied. Finding someone with whom you can be totally honest is no small feat. And, of course, supervision doesn't fully work without this complete honesty. There have been times in my career when I have found supervision to be a profound relief, offering me perspective and insight about both my blind spots and my strengths. There have been other times when I have experienced strong feelings of defensiveness and shame in supervision. Without supervision, I could have never properly terminated with Rita. With other clients, the clinical work has led to a demise in the supervision because of strong conflicts between my belief system and that of the supervisor and a shared anxiety around ethical struggles. For better and worse, supervision is where a lot of work is. It is a vulnerable, essential, and organizing destination for us to make meaning of our most difficult struggles and to ask our deepest questions.

Supervision is an often undervalued, yet paramount, element of clinical social work. Our field, largely informed by classroom teaching, relies heavily on the sharing of practice wisdom between generations. This is what differentiates our functioning as a field from many others.

Supervision is founded upon the notion that there is no better classroom than the field itself, and there is no better teacher in that classroom than the most experienced and actively practicing social worker. Many schools of social work employ professors who are researchers, rather than practitioners. However, it is understood that central aspects of social work education are imparted from clinician to clinician.

Surrendering oneself to the process of supervision is one of the most difficult elements of our professional development. Supervision can be humbling, embarrassing, sometimes shaming, bolstering, empowering, and profoundly relieving. Supervision doesn't always feel good, and it isn't necessarily supposed to. It is designed to get clinicians to truly look at themselves, at their blind spots, and at their knowledge gaps. Supervision is sometimes organized around the sharing of a process recording, but more often than not, supervision happens when the supervisee tells his or her story of what occurred in a clinical encounter.

Supervision relies on our vulnerable truth telling and guidance seeking. This is a tenuous position for a new employee, and takes a lot of relearning the rules of what it means to be a "good" professional, because growth can only occur at the admittance of our own mistakes. The idea of openly sharing mistakes with our bosses, administrators, and leaders is certainly counterintuitive and nothing short of essential if we are to grow. Learning how to be in supervision is a central developmental task in becoming a clinical social worker.

Following graduation, entering effective supervision is a complicated endeavor, made all the more complicated when seeking licensure. The role of the student in supervision is a unique one from which it is difficult to break free. As a student, you are in the clear position of receiving information from your supervisor, and adjustments for your mistakes are made psychologically by the agency as a whole. When you are a student, your supervision is clearly designed to impart practice wisdom, to aid in intellectual development, and to make sure that work is happening in accordance with agency policy and in the best interest of the clients.

Once you have your MSW, this dynamic ought to shift. Getting out of the role of the student and becoming the consumer of supervision is a difficult shift to make. It means surrendering the notion that supervision serves as a type of "confessional" aided, as it is in school, by the use of process recordings. Supervision ought to become more collegial, should assist in the development of consolidating gains in the process of theory acquisition, might be part business mentorship, and should ultimately serve as a home for the creation of solid case conceptualization.

Included in this chapter is advice on finding the "right" supervisor. However, if that supervisor is assigned as part of one's employment, advice on how to maximize perceived "mismatches" between supervisor and supervisee will be addressed. I will examine steps toward the co-creation of case conceptualization, and explore what is appropriate fodder for supervision versus therapy. The goal for new social workers is to celebrate supervision rather than to fear it—to use it rather than to coast through it. Also in this chapter, I have included social workers' accounts of their supervision experiences. These social workers shared their experiences through a survey of 100 social workers that I conducted to gather information for this book.

My wish for all social workers is that your agency provides you with solid supervision upon graduation. Having to find a supervisor outside of your work setting can be costly and time consuming. That said, it can also have some tremendous benefits—giving you the opportunity to speak with someone not tied to the politics of your agency, someone with whom you feel theoretical synchronicity, and someone who can follow you through various professional endeavors rather than simply the job where you are currently employed.

In-Agency Supervision

Let's first discuss what you can and should expect from in-agency supervision. Before getting started in any new position, you should get a clear understanding of how supervision will happen. Will it happen as needed? Will it happen weekly? Is there group supervision? Peer supervision (not led by an experienced clinician)? If you do get supervision, is it provided by an LCSW (or equivalent in your state) or another licensed professional whose supervisory hours will aid you in the process of acquiring licensure? When discussing salary and benefits, these are questions that you need to ask, because this is part of your benefits package, and it is an essential part of how you are going to get advanced licensure in the future.

The frequency of supervision in an agency varies considerably. For the most part, supervision is supposed to happen weekly, but that does not always appear to be the case. Although the majority receive supervision weekly, in or out of an agency setting, some social workers suggest that they are receiving supervision monthly or bi-monthly. One social worker describes the ambiguity of supervisory structure in her agency: "My director has an open door policy, so I staff when needed, but officially once per month."

However often in-agency supervision occurs, it is basically designed to be an "overseeing process." There are three dimensions of your work that should be overseen. These are administrative, educational, and support for your clinical work. These three elements co-occur and do overlap and should all be present in the supervisory relationship.

The Administrative Dimension

Administrative supervision aids in the promotion of sustenance of agency standards. It helps you to become oriented to agency policy and how to act in accordance with it. It also ensures that you have enough time in your schedule to adhere to what is expected of you.

My first post-master's job was in a college counseling center. I got excellent clinical supervision, but I never discussed in supervision ways of managing my time while adhering to the required administrative duties. As a result, I never truly developed the important ability to document my work well and to write progress notes in a way that would allow for seamless agency functioning. This is not the fault of the agency or the supervisor. It is simply very difficult to make use of supervision and make sure that all areas of your professional identity are being attended to.

One clinical social worker articulates this phenomenon with great clarity: "I am a new employee, under a new supervisor. My agency is so fast-paced that there was absolutely no time for orientation. Learning on the job is proving quite a challenge, especially when my supervisor is also learning." Another social worker echoes this stress, saying, "My supervision is given by a non-clinical social worker who meets with me on occasion or when I beg for it."

Essentially, the primary goal of the administrative element of your supervision is to ensure your ability to adhere to agency policy and procedure. Ideally, this should occupy about 10% of your time in supervision. There is certainly supervision that becomes focused on the administrative aspects of your work to a fault, and this risk must also be carefully monitored as you seek to grow in the field.

The administrative dimension of supervision includes support with time management, support in treatment planning, clarification of note writing skills, policy adherence, and information on proper intake and assessment technique. If the administrative dimension seems to be missing from your supervision, you need to become very clear about what you feel you are lacking. With this in mind, you can arrive for supervision highly prepared with a list of clear questions about agency policy, paperwork guidelines, and general inquiries about agency culture and functioning.

We often become extremely inhibited when we have a question for which we believe we should have the answer. In the more administrative components of supervision, this "hiding" of questions that feel inane, or obvious, can become highly insidious. Having a question about paperwork or documentation is often of equal import to having a question about an elusive diagnosis. Proceeding with a sense of incompetence about how to function administratively can become very destabilizing in any position. Ask your questions in a highly organized and structured way, knowing that every question you have is only going to help you to perform at a higher level once it is answered.

The Educational Dimension

Educational supervision is best described as the element of supervision that enables the supervisee to better understand the client. The goal of the educational part of supervision is to help social workers to develop their full potential as diagnosticians, assessors, and clinicians who are able to form strong and powerful therapeutic alliances.

When presenting a client, the supervisee should be aided in the process of making links, discovering patterns, and identifying specific symptoms that can be categorized and understood diagnostically. The social worker must be encouraged to realize his or her usefulness and impact on clients' lives. Many new social workers are understandably naïve, if not blind to the strong impact that they have on clients' lives. It often takes a senior social worker to identify how this impact is occurring and to enlighten the social worker to the power, influence, and meaning that he or she has.

Other elements of the educational dimension of supervision include aiding the social worker in the development of a stronger comprehension of the relational dynamics that are informing the treatment. Supervisees should be supported in their efforts to better understand their responses to a client. Supervisees should also be provided the space to articulate why they chose a specific intervention and to examine the outcomes associated with that choice. And perhaps most importantly, supervisees, through the process of good supervision, can begin to incubate the important capacity to recognize their own patterns of clinical behavior, for both better and worse.

The educational elements of supervision are undoubtedly difficult. For supervision to become educational, the supervisee needs to trust the supervisor's opinion, experience, and knowledge. The supervisee has to also, frankly, be willing to say anything to the supervisor. And this is just incredibly hard. The ability to talk openly with a supervisor is what allows authentic education to happen, and it also takes a tremendous amount of time to build up that level of trust in a supervisor.

Paramount to building this type of trust is a significant amount of self-awareness. When a clinician isn't telling the supervisor something, it is not always necessary to just come out and say. Rather, the process of trying to understand the ambivalence and sharing that ambivalence is what builds a strong and educational supervisory relationship.

The Supportive Dimension

Supervision must have strong supportive dimensions. The supportive aspects of supervision ought to be organized around managing the worker's stress, working through and regulating intense experiences of vicarious traumatization, and helping the worker to make adjustments in his or her work to create professional stamina and sustainability. Supervision should be a space in which social workers derive energy, and this energy is directly correlated with the level of positive support that is offered in supervision.

There is not a huge distinction between the educational and supportive aspects of supervision. However, the educational elements are more instructive, whereas the supportive piece allows for the social worker's own self-exploration and development.

Supportive supervision is best organized around the important work of understanding and distinguishing between issues of content versus process. Social workers, like all people, are simply drawn to content and often quite stirred up by it. Content is absolutely important, but supervision should allow a social worker to reflect on the delivery of the content, the patterns embedded in the content, and the latent meaning of the content. It takes a strongly supportive guide to shift one's thinking from content (where all of the gravity appears to be) to the process, which requires a level of skill and critical thought that takes years to become attuned to.

Important, too, in the reception of supportive supervision is the need to be validated as both a social worker and a human. This seems almost elementary to say, but excellent supervision reminds us of our complexity and vulnerability as people in the world. The pressures of our work, conversely, encourage us to forget these realities. Supportive supervision aids the social worker in developing a keen eye toward his or her own blind spots and defensive functioning without putting the worker on the defensive.

The supervision should also ensure that there is someone to share the psychological burden of the projections, traumas, and generally difficult material that arises with some of our clients. This shared burden paves the way for social workers to truly examine their own countertransference reactions and the ways in which the work might be triggering for them. In many ways, the supportive elements of supervision feel the most like therapy. Yet, the irony is that the strength of the supervision is determined by the supervisor's ability to hold tenuous yet essential boundaries, empowering the social worker to seek therapy in a way that is devoid of shame and instead imbued with pride and self-care.

Maximizing Mismatches

Inevitably, upon receiving in-agency supervision, some social workers will experience a sense of clinical and ideological mismatch with their supervisors. And it's okay. The key to surviving these perceived mismatches is to clearly articulate your experience of them.

For example, you might have a supervisor who believes wholeheartedly in the curative nature of self disclosure. For you, this simply might not resonate. You have to say that. You and your supervisor need to cultivate a respectable way of negotiating and accepting your differences.

I had a supervisor term the potential of our differences as productive challenges. This feels like a highly relevant term for what will often, if you allow it to occur, happen in supervision.

A supervisory mismatch is only equated to failure when our response to it is to present a false clinical self to obscure the reality of our clinical differences. And, in fact, the central risk to a mismatch is that it can perpetuate our feelings of having a false professional self. This is a huge danger for new social workers. We already feel burdened by our lack of experience, by the hierarchical structure of our agencies, and by a constant sense of not knowing. We spend a lot of time endorsing the old adage, "Fake it 'til you make it." Feeling theoretically or clinically misattuned with a supervisor can extend one's use of this adage into the supervision room. This should not happen.

Supervision is the space to surrender your "act," to ask every question you have, and to acknowledge your struggles. The goal is not to please or mirror your supervisor. The goal is to grow and to help your clients grow. Making your experience in supervision completely transparent, even if you feel wildly different from your supervisor, will allow you to at least practice the skills you need to have difficult conversations, individuate from superiors, and find your authentic voice.

Group Supervision and Peer Supervision

Many agencies offer group and peer supervision as either a replacement for individual supervision or as an adjunct to it. The important distinction between group supervision and peer supervision is that group supervision ought to be led by an experienced clinician. Peer supervision is defined by its lack of direct leadership, relying instead on the equality of the group process.

The strength of group and peer supervision can lie in the interdisciplinary presence of different professionals. Many strong supervision groups are populated by psychiatrists, psychologists, and social workers. More diverse settings include other mental health professionals, such as psychiatric nurse practitioners, licensed marriage and family therapists, mental health counselors, and art therapists. The more perspectives that are brought into group supervision, the richer the conversation can be.

The problem with interdisciplinary group supervision for social workers is that, hierarchically, we are not always as valued professionally. Watching this reality enacted in a supervisory setting can be very painful. Maximizing the experience of group supervision requires a precise understanding of the value of our perspective and offering this perspective. Many times, group supervision can become fixated on diagnosis and is bent toward the medical model. Part of our role as social workers is to become activists in situations in which the whole of the client is not being adequately addressed.

Receiving half of your supervision in the form of group supervision does aid in the licensure process, but your group supervision must happen concurrently with individual supervision for those hours to count. It is possible that this rule varies from state to state, and you must check with your local licensing body to confirm this information, as requirements are frequently shifting. Following licensure, it is not uncommon for individual supervision to end while we remain in group and peer supervision. The isolation of dealing dyadically with clients is often wonderfully remedied through the group supervision process.

Out-of-Agency/Private Supervision

Seeking out-of-agency supervision is an empowering, sometimes expensive, and often necessary process. The fact of the matter is that many professional settings simply don't offer regular supervision. Further, agencies often do not provide the specific type or amount of supervision that is required in your state for licensure. Agencies are almost unilaterally strapped for time and resources, and the first resource that often gets the short shrift is supervision. Supervisors, bowing to multiple systemic demands, are often forced to make supervision a secondary priority. That can be frustrating, but in many ways it is an opportunity to strike out on your own and find supervision that truly suits your needs.

The first step in seeking supervision for yourself is to set a budget. Finding a supervisor that you can't afford is frustrating and disappointing. There are, in many cities, lists of supervisors who have agreed to see beginning clinicians at reduced rates. Making your identity known, as a newly employed social worker, is an essential part of your process, because many senior clinicians are willing to find ways of working with newer clinicians.

Next, you want to think about and become clear on whether you want a supervisor who is closely aligned with a particular theoretical orientation. This is total fair game for your search process and ought to be highly prioritized. Few clinicians practice with orthodoxy, meaning a strict adherence to one way of practicing or thinking. However, if you are seeking to grow as a psychodynamic clinician, seeing a supervisor who practices behaviorally will leave you feeling stunted. This is very much an interview process with you as the consumer. Shop for what you need, and know what to ask.

When meeting supervisors, ask them who most informs their thinking, what writings they hold most closely, and what social work values guide them most closely. Ask your potential supervisors to tell you about their predominant client base. Ask your potential supervisors if they have a sliding scale, enabling them to see a wider socioeconomic base of clients. Ask your potential supervisors if process recordings are part of the supervision process, and depending on whether or not this works for you, take this information seriously. Ask your potential supervisors what their stance is on self disclosure and how they understand their use of self. This may feel like a lot of questions, but this is a decision that must be made in a highly informed manner.

Notice, of course, that I placed matching theoretical orientation above matching experience with treatment population or treatment setting. For example, you might be starting out in a drug and alcohol setting and hoping to find a clinician with experience in this specific area. That is an excellent goal—primary, in fact. However, I would suggest that it is slightly secondary to sharing a theoretical perspective. This is mainly because a shared theoretical perspective will allow you to build a supervisory relationship that spans many career shifts, rather than providing support for the exact job you are in at any given moment.

Other important questions to ask are: What types of settings have you worked in? Do you have experience negotiating complicated agency dynamics? Have you worked with children, adults, groups, or couples? If there does appear to be a professional discrepancy in terms of experience, it does not mean that the supervision won't work. It is perfectly acceptable to ask your potential supervisor how he or she perceives the discrepancy and observe the supervisor's comfort level with possibly needing to grow together.

Another element of clarification when seeking a supervisory fit is: How do you and how does your potential supervisor understand the role of supervision? Many people use supervision as a confessional—a superego of sorts. Others use it for theory development. Others use it for case conceptualization. Others use it as a guide through complex bureaucratic and systemic issues. There is no right or wrong answer—the hope is for there to be some overlap between your vision and the supervisor's. It is important for both you and the supervisor to clearly articulate what your visions of the work are, even if those visions are intentionally ambiguous and that feels right.

Supervision is like therapy in that it ought to evolve organically. However, there ought to also be a mutual understanding of the expectations of the supervision. Supervision is also a bit like school, and your learning style, along with your supervisor's teaching style, both really matter. If you are a kinesthetic learner and your supervisor is more of a lecturer, this can be a problematic fit.

For example, I have a supervisee whose past supervisor was only willing to work with her around process recordings. They would go through the process recordings line by line, and it was torturous for the supervisee. She felt ashamed and intensely scrutinized. She also felt as if her memory was not reliable enough to even create process recordings worthy of this level of dissection. I, on the other hand, prefer supervision that focused on very minute pieces of process. It gives me a sense of what is going on through the study of microcosmic interactions. It also gives me insight into a lot of what is happening unconsciously that I might be missing.

Good supervision is based on a good alignment. But even better supervision is based on the transparency on the part of both parties about all of the different ways that each person learns and is able to listen.

Last, I would suggest discussing the role of personal information in supervision. Some supervisors have a high tolerance for a blurred role between supervision and therapy; others prefer much more clarity. Again, there isn't a right or wrong way here. As part of your role as a consumer of supervision, this is simply important information to know. Discussing your own countertransferential responses in supervision is an essential part of the growth process, and understanding the structure and boundaries around this process with your supervisor is an important task in terms of moving the supervision forward.

Seeking Outside Group and Peer Supervision

No matter how wonderful the supervisory opportunities are at your agency, the possibilities presented to you by attending local group or peer supervision outside of your agency are incalculable. Group supervision exposes you to group process, a central element in terms of your lifelong training. Group supervision also exposes you to different aspects of the field. I currently run a supervision group that represents five very distinct settings: school social work, medical social work, drug and alcohol treatment, college counseling, and geriatric social work. The beauty in the distinction is the strong overlap in experiences. The deeper beauty, though, is the exposure to the broad and different ways that social work is lived and performed. Staying informed about the field as a whole keeps you abreast of evolutions in the field, recent advances in best practices, and evidence-based techniques. It also helps you determine whether you might have a burgeoning interest in new areas of practice.

Group supervision outside of your agency also allows you to truly discuss the complex and intricate dynamics of your workplace without compromising any professional relationships. There is rarely an exception to the rule that agencies function in highly politicized and thorny ways. Respite from the unrelenting nature of that reality is part of the self-preservation process. Group supervision offers you the opportunity for full disclosure of your frustrations and your triumphs in a uniquely confidential and safe atmosphere. Successful supervision groups can be long-term, some lasting for more than 20 years. This can be a space for you to develop lifelong collegial relationships, for you to form connections in a new city or town, and for you to assure that your growth is not bound by the limitations of your current work situation.

A fellow social worker stated about group supervision: "I meet with a group twice a month and find it a critical piece of loving what I do. I also meet with peers once per month in a group. If I had more time and money, I think individual supervision would be helpful." In fact, the need for peer support through outside supervision was articulated by more than 70% of the clinical social workers surveyed for this book.

Another social worker states, "My [agency] supervisor is a Ph.D. in nothing related to social work, so I have a group of clinical social workers from every aspect of the field that I consult with." These emblematic thoughts emphasize the need to meet not only with clinically-minded people, but also specifically with other *social workers* who are well versed in numerous areas of the profession. These articulations also suggest a powerful and underlying human need for companionship and understanding that comes from meeting with one's peers.

It also seems that with more experience, the comfort with peer supervision versus group supervision grows. One social worker states: "I personally attend a supervision group once a month and seek outside consultation as needed. In school, we had a 'group' supervision biweekly, which is not true supervision. I find peer supervision and informal supervision with other social workers much more helpful." This informality and comfort, offered by peer supervision, greatly lends itself to a sense of sustainability in the field that few other forms of supervision can in the same energizing way.

Are social workers getting supervision?

In my survey of 100 clinical social workers, the majority receive supervision only in a group setting. Only 15% report receiving individual supervision in-agency, and this supervision is predominantly received on an as-needed basis or is used as a form of informal consultation. Of the 15% who do receive in-agency supervision, just under half are satisfied with that supervision. Twenty-five percent of respondents stated that there is a need to go outside of their work settings to procure the individual supervision they desire. This suggests that about a quarter of us are paying for supervision. This also suggests that there is somewhat of a crisis around supervision in the field and that part of our work, as social workers, is to turn the tide back to a valuing of supervision.

Supervision and the sharing of knowledge is a central strength of our field, often offsetting many of the disadvantages of social work. Although social work may not pay very well and is emotionally taxing, the intellectual stimulation, collegiality, and support that come with supervision often can offset these other stressors. Also, supervision can exist in many forms, as widely voiced by social workers in the field. One social worker writes, "I have group clinical supervision once weekly (I pay). I receive group trainings and/or supervision once per month from my agency, and individual supervision is available per request." The possibilities for how supervision happens and in what form are certainly, and fortunately, countless.

Is supervision helpful/necessary?

In agencies, 20% of the clinical social workers surveyed find supervision to be helpful, and only 4% consider it to be vital. About 10% of these social workers are dissatisfied with their supervision because of the overly administrative nature of it. This reflects a very problematic reality, which is that in-agency supervision is frequently bound to managing agencies' concerns, meeting charting requirements, and servicing insurance companies. As mentioned, these are central parts of the supervisory process, but they should not eclipse the educational and supportive pieces of supervision. The dissatisfaction with in-agency supervision exists across multiple social work settings, including government agencies, colleges, schools, private practice, and community mental health centers. Social workers from all of these settings articulated a total lack of supervision or the minimal availability of it.

One clinical social worker stated, "Individual supervision is often interrupted by my supervisor's numerous agency responsibilities. Supervision is very task oriented, rather than process oriented." This illustrates some of the barriers of agency settings and quality supervision. Additionally, this suggests that supervision is sometimes a low priority at the agency level.

Another social worker said, "I have just started regular individual supervisory meetings after six months at the agency. It is mostly about administrative issues: charting, procedures, doing assessments, training on computer software. There is a monthly staff meeting. No good clinical supervision." This also raises the issues of a high-paced, high-pressure setting. Procedure and tasks, charting, and electronic medical records trump the basic need of new social workers to obtain the clinical supervision they require. Six months of work without any supervision suggests the agency places a low priority on supervision in general, and the understanding of what supervision is and/or should be is narrowed to technical issues.

Another respondent stated that she does "meet regularly for individual supervision. Supervision is not effective, because the supervisor is not well equipped to provide clinical supervision."

Struggles with the strength of the supervisory alliance are thematically present in the field, echoed by the following: "Individual supervision is not helpful [because of my] poor rapport with my supervisor. We spend supervision learning how to do better 'assessment' rather than processing clinical development/countertransference." Having the self-awareness to know that your own developmental issues ought to be part of your supervision is paramount to trying to make this happen.

These complex supervisory issues, which occur in-agency, are symptomatic of an under-resourced field. That should not deter you from self-advocacy. Advocating for your own excellent supervision is advocating for your clients, knowing that their growth rests on your growth.

Although there are clear stressors in the realm of in-agency supervision, those receiving private supervision reported nearly universal rates of satisfaction with it. Perhaps this is an issue of "you get what you pay for." Data suggest that it is more than that, though. Satisfaction with private supervision relates to the need to discuss complex issues outside of a work setting that is saturated with hierarchy and workplace politics (Frawley-O'Dea & Sarnat, 2001). There appears to be a minimal presence of shame in private supervision, whereas the role of shame looms quite large when your supervisor is also your employer, and your livelihood partly rests on your confessions.

Early Career Supervision Versus Your Seasoned Years

It can be well argued that the need for supervision lasts for the duration of one's career. The nature of the need does shift, though. A wise clinical social worker writes, "I have hired a consultant to work with, who has been in the field [many years]. I had supervision all the way from the very beginning, through master's, internships, and currently I always consult with others. I don't ever feel as though I know all the answers, and clearly two heads are better than one."

The eternal need for supervision exists because we need different things at different stages of our careers. When first seeking supervision, it is to form an identity as a therapist. In the middle phase of your career, it is to become a master of your own blind spots. And ironically, supervision in the later years of your career is about de-solidifying your clinical social worker identity and recognizing the essential need for constant broadening of style and technique. Perhaps, better stated, there is a difference between the supervision one obtains at the beginning of one's career, which can be very "problem" focused, and the supervision one obtains toward the end of a career, which becomes more "process" focused.

Further, late career supervision also enhances our ability to provide excellent supervision ourselves. One social worker articulates the interminable need to better understand our work, while also providing supervision to others: "I am in weekly clinical supervision, which is enriching to my understanding of clinical work and development as a psychotherapist. I also provide weekly clinical supervision to newly licensed or provisionally licensed social workers."

Another social worker discussed the sustaining quality of later career supervision and the growing casual nature of the need. "At this point in my career, supervision is more informal. I do see my supervisor daily, and when we meet, it is usually to discuss specific issues (not necessarily problems). We discuss processes and how we are going to meet goals of the organization and provide the right care at the right time. We also process therapy groups after group."

In considering the expiration of the need for supervision, the following thoughts were shared: "I am a senior clinician. I have sporadic consultation and supervision as needed." "I am a supervisor." "I've been in practice for more than 34 years. I no longer am in supervision. I supervise others." "I no longer receive supervision, although I did have many years of...supervision."

Perhaps it is true that we age out of the need for supervision—it probably varies from clinician to clinician. However, the point at which we meet the requirements for licensure—a tempting supervisory endpoint—is simply quite early in one's career to stop seeking growth in this way. As consumers of supervision, I would encourage you to not let any licensing board determine the length and extent of your supervisory needs. I would also encourage you to proceed as an empowered, informed, and confident consumer who knows that this investment is an investment in every client you have.

Chapter 12
If I Had Known Then:
Adventures From the First Years

This chapter will explore some of the themes that come up for social workers, both neophyte and veteran. First there are narratives of the experience of the first year out. I will then go into some of the themes that social workers have articulated that they wish they had known entering the field. Maybe this is a cheat sheet, or just what an older sibling would give a kid sister or brother going to sleep away camp for the first time.

The First Year

The first year out of graduate school in social work is a very complicated one, often haunted by moments of disillusionment and fear. The search for a job, itself, is a daunting task. Although some students are able to secure employment at their second-year field placements, things don't always work out that seamlessly. Some students spend several months looking for a job. I have seen graduates apply for anywhere from five to 250 jobs. In some areas, the job market is saturated. In others, it is not. It can be very hard to apply for a job without a license. However, in some cases, this is a non-issue.

It is essential to realize that your first job out of school does not need to be perfect. I do believe that it has to be at least somewhat educational, meaning that the inclusion of supervision or some sort of in-service trainings on a regular basis is completely fair to expect.

I also think it is important to take on a lot, but if something feels unmanageable in terms of your development, it is essential to pay attention to this. Sustainability in the field of clinical social work is a very delicate issue, and the pacing of your energy as a social worker has to be something that you think about as you plan your career. It seems so trite to say, but in this field, the idea of training for a marathon versus a sprint is a very powerful metaphor.

I think it is also important to consider when you are going to begin your job search. For financial reasons, certainly, some begin their search early. However, I can tell you after having taught many second-year practice students that it is seriously worth considering how you will protect yourself from the virally anxious atmosphere that ensues during the last term of the second year of MSW programs. There is a tremendous amount of competition for jobs and to have a job. Insulating yourself from this is part of a long-range planning technique for surviving in the field in general. A lot goes on in a viral manner psychologically that is anxiety-provoking and draining. I would argue that making plans for preserving an emotional acre of land for yourself will be key to your long-range survival as a social worker.

In the following anecdote, one of my supervisees describes her experience one year out of school. In it, you will find some powerful and familiar themes–most specifically, the struggle to maintain an individual identity in a powerful agency culture and the struggle to know whether or not "real" change is occurring for clients.

Victoria—The Reality

My job search began even before graduate school ended. My finances after graduating were tight, and I took the first job I was offered at a nursing home outside the city. I applied for many jobs, over fifty, before being offered one. I was called for an interview at a handful of jobs, and felt comfortable that the job I took was in the field I wanted to be in–geriatrics. In general, though, I found the job search to be disheartening. It was difficult to find a job in the location that I wanted to be in, for a salary I could live [on], and for an agency I believed in.

When I entered my position, I now realize that I was naïve in my thinking. I came to work with the idea that employees show up to do their jobs and act professionally while doing so. However, what I realized during my first year of work is that the workplace is filled with drama. I have felt very unsettled with that aspect of coming to work. I have also had my eyes opened as a medical social worker, realizing that many things are done for money and not for the well-being of the individual. People are a commodity in health care, and that is something I cannot get on board with. I have had to do things that I don't necessarily agree with, which forces me to consistently ask myself why I got into social work in the first place and question whether what I am doing aligns with those reasons.

I have felt very confident in my role as a case manager, and the longer I work, the more comfortable I feel with family meetings and client interactions. However, as far as clinical practice with clients goes, I am still working to feel comfortable. I feel confident in my diagnostic skills, but my intervention skills are what I feel are lacking. I am still skeptical of myself and whether or not I am really "helping" people. I have received appreciation notes and other validation in my work, but I still question myself at times.

In general, social work has turned out to be somewhat as I imagined it would be. I do get satisfaction from my interactions with residents and their families. However, I didn't realize that I would have to give so many messages that I don't believe in, especially when working for a nonprofit organization. I didn't realize that I would have to work so hard for the bottom line and seemingly less hard for the clients themselves. I often feel stuck in my role as someone working for the organization but also for the clients as their advocate. It is hard to feel unhappy in a job and yet afraid to leave because the job search was so daunting the first time around. I don't regret my decision to become a social worker. If anything, I feel after working in the field that it is an even more valuable career.

Victoria is referring to a very powerful growing awareness of the needs of her clients and the drive of her agency. Her despair about this mismatch grew, but this also fueled in her an even deeper belief in the necessity of our work.

Mia—It Gets Better

Mia, another supervisee of mine, recognized almost immediately that she was in a setting that was making her hate her work and hate the field. This certainly happens. It was an essential piece of our supervision to get Mia to surrender the random dictum that you need to stay in a job for a year before you can look elsewhere. Staying in any toxic environment for an extended period of time will hurt your ability to survive in this field over the long term. She wrote:

When I was in school, both undergrad and graduate, I always preferred field work to class. Obviously, when I graduated from grad school, I thought being in the field full time as a professional would come naturally. When I first started my job, I was so excited. The job was not the population I wanted to work with, but it gave me a great opportunity to work on my group therapy skills, which were definitely lacking. The job was as a group therapist working with adult men with mental illness and sexual deviancy. It was awful. After my first week, I started looking for other jobs. It was difficult getting through the content of the groups at first, but once I got past that and got in the groove of groups, I had no support.

The other therapists were good work friends who also hated their jobs, but my supervisor was not present physically and mentally. I never had supervision in the four months I worked there. I started feeling anxious about going to work and completely drowning emotionally. One week, I was in the office at 7:00 or 7:30 each morning and worked through the small lunch break I got. That Thursday night, I had cried myself to sleep because I hated the job so much. I felt so unhealthy emotionally and physically. I cried as I walked to work the next morning, and that's when I decided I was done. I handed in my notice and was gone in one month.

During this time and afterwards, I went through a whirlwind of emotions. I felt shame, guilt, excitement, happiness, and pride. The guilt and shame took over the others, because I felt as if I had failed and let down myself, people I cared about, and social work. The next four months were exhausting, but nowhere near as awful as I felt at my job.

The job search was draining. Each day, I would go on CareerBuilder, Indeed, and various agency websites and robotically rewrite and submit my résumé. There was so much rejection. I finally got job offers. After four months of not working and approximately a year of submitting résumés, I had offers for two jobs I didn't want. One was with a nursing home, which made me so uncomfortable, and the second offer was my current job. When I got the call from my supervisor, it was a rainy day after Valentine's Day....

Now I am working somewhere with full-time support from co-workers and my supervisor. It's not the ideal job or where I want to stay permanently. However, I am working on my clinical hours and learning about a new field that I had no experience with and am tremendously enjoying. Now I feel as if I need more of the classwork that I was not as comfortable with in order to continue learning what I'm not necessarily gaining at my job.

The first year after graduate school was challenging on many levels, exciting, and just depressing at some times, but it did get better—a crazy amount better!

Mia fell into many of the traps that new graduates do, through no fault of her own. First, and for no understandable reason, new graduates are often put into jobs that are heavily focused on some—if not all—group work. Group work is extremely challenging and complicated, and many new graduates are not well prepared for it. I don't, myself, have a good understanding of why this work is given to the newest members of our field. I do know that it can accelerate burnout, and it is a disservice to clients and clinicians alike when the clinicians are not prepared for or supported in this work.

Secondly, it is often the newer graduates who are skipped over when it comes to supervision hours. I am not sure if this is because agencies that are feeling strapped and overwhelmed have an unconscious sense that newer graduates/newer employees have less of an ability to advocate for themselves, or if this is just a sheer coincidence. Either way, the powerful and disturbing material that Mia was working with clinically was completely unmitigated by any sort of support. I am not suggesting there was a way for Mia to get around this—there are simply toxic work environments.

I do think that if a workplace suggests that you will spend most of your time doing groups, it is fair to say, "That's great. Do you have any resources or materials on how groups are run in this setting or with this population?" Portraying a false sense of knowing to get a job is a completely understandable tendency, and we do have to sell ourselves. But we don't have to sell ourselves into situations that we can't realistically manage. And it is okay—really okay—to be honest about what we know and don't know in an interview, and to be honest about the fact that our learning process is ongoing.

Aisha—The Let-Downs

Aisha, another member of my supervision group, spoke to the complexities of her first year out of school:

One thing I wish I had known prior to entering the field is how little respect I believe social workers receive. I think about the perception people have of social workers—that we all work for DHS and take children away. This has even contributed to my desire never to work at DHS and be overworked. Little did I know that even with the title of therapist, I am underappreciated. Working in an agency has shown me how much psychiatrists are respected and how their role is senior compared to mine as a therapist. This all boils down to less pay in many sectors of the behavioral/mental health fields.

I was disappointed with the job postings, because I was looking for something similar to what I was doing before I attended graduate school. The state mental health [system] is different from the state where I lived previously, and it felt as if I was being pushed into behavioral health and CBT. Then I found out that there is only one payer for all the state-funded services. It all made sense. I could easily get SOME type of job (and I needed to so that I could eat), but I felt that I wouldn't be satisfied.

Another disappointment was the way hiring requirements are set up. You cannot do anything without the MSW, but in some cases, you must also have one to two years of post-graduate experience for some tasks. This leaves new graduates out in the cold. That did not make sense to me. I thought this was part of the reason we had field placements.

So, I started working at a few agencies simultaneously—ones that I thought I could tolerate. I felt confident prior to entering graduate school and even more so after my second-year field placement, because that is when I gained most of my experience.

This isn't all of what I imagined it would be. I feel like a volunteer for what little money I make. I expected to be able to eat well, have benefits, have entertainment, take a vacation, buy a home, and save some money.

Aisha is speaking to many, many complex let-downs that face first-year graduates. First, there are complex licensing restrictions that make the job search feel unbelievably opaque and difficult to navigate. It turns out that the MSW is just the first of many hurdles toward practicing freely. This is something that is difficult for graduates to get information about and that schools don't necessarily spend a lot of time discussing. It is important to become a part of your state NASW chapter, particularly as a student (at a discounted rate), to start becoming educated on licensure and other professional realities in your jurisdiction.

Aisha also took a route that many graduates take, which is the piecing together of many part-time jobs. There is nothing inherently good or bad about this choice, with the exception of the fact that it makes health insurance much harder to secure. The advantage, though, is that this is often a route toward exposure to different treatment populations. This allows you to figure out what works for you—what feels most right. It also sets you up for a full-time job that you can feel more sure about.

Aisha is also referencing another highly painful reality. That is how hierarchically structured agencies can feel and how painful it can feel to be on the bottom of so many professional totem poles. It is true—this feeling is often there, and there is no sugar coating it.

There are a lot of ways to make sense of it, to make use of it, to interpret it. For me, I have often considered this reality to be a way to better understand the struggles of oppressed clients. It may seem ridiculous to say, but in many ways, always feeling "less than" or "inferior to" in a professional environment can be a useful and consistent empathy builder. I also think about it in terms of defensive functioning. Why is social work so low on the totem pole? Perhaps this sounds crazy, but I believe it is because we are really onto something. I believe that the depths of the relationships that we form with clients are incomparably powerful and transformative and that this fact is threatening on a deeply psychic level to other professionals. I think that our internal knowing and claiming of this possibility can give us great sustenance and clarity. Still, it does not right the wrongs of our experiences of disempowerment.

Jenn—The Firsts

Jenn, like Aisha, Mia, and Victoria, had a volatile first year out of school. Listen to what she had to say:

Everything is a first. If I could go back to the beginning of my social work job search and to the first year of my social work career, I would tell myself exactly that–everything is a first. Your first drafts of a social work résumé, your first interview as an MSW, your first meeting with a family, your first crisis. While graduate school and previous experiences in the field and in internships are great at giving you a foundation, you really start to learn and grow as a social worker in those first few months. You learn the real importance of boundaries and self-care. It is no longer the process recording or the 10-page paper. It is real life. Whether you work with families, adults, the elderly, or children, people put trust in you—not your supervisor or professor—and all the things you studied suddenly become real.

The reality of working took time to set in, and not for the reason one might imagine. It took time for me, because the job search itself is a full-time job. Five months and 65 job applications later, I found my job–gratefully, a job worth waiting for. I applied only to jobs that appealed to me at first, and then to others outside of my interests, because I started to feel desperate. But now having a job I love, I realize that the wait is worth it. I would not have been able to support myself financially or emotionally with some of the jobs I interviewed for. It seems basic, or perhaps from a Social Work 101 class, but if I can't maintain who I am, I will definitely not be able to help my clients.

Once I started work, I quickly realized how strict I had to be in setting my own boundaries with clients, their families, and colleagues. Surprisingly, I found it most difficult with my colleagues. I needed to be clear in my role to make sure I could do it well. I also had to make sure I didn't bring my "stuff" from the field home with me to my friends and family. It's almost like trying to piece a puzzle together until you figure out how to make social work the career you wanted and also be able to maintain it. My best tool was using my commute to work as a mental preparation and the way home for reflection. It allows me time to prepare and digest so I continue to live the other chapters of my life outside of work.

Social work was a change in careers for me, and I now know what it is like to wake up in the morning and want to go to work. While it may be frustrating and tiring, the job search process is worth it when you find a job you like and feel supported in. Luckily, for me, a career in social work is what I expected. My clients keep me fresh every day, and I get constant reminders that in clinical jobs, there is always more to learn.

I think that Jenn speaks beautifully to the need for creative survival strategies in the field. First, she clearly delineates just how different the school world and the real world feel, and it's true. Once you realize that there is no professor to grade you or supervisor to sign off—just a client or a family waiting on your opinion, your judgment, your guidance, your support—the game feels tremendously different. And this does seep in.

Social workers think and talk all the time about self-care and boundary setting. We talk about it in ways that are both big and small. What I love so much about what Jenn says is that she uses her commute. It is so simple and elegant. It is affordable and doable. And it works. There are these simple preservative measures that we can take that enhance the sustainability of our time in the field, and I think she speaks to the dual feasibility and necessity of this.

Julia—Emotional Boot Camp

I wish I had known how emotionally draining this work really is. Of course, they can try to prepare you for this aspect of the profession in school. However, until you are in it, there is no way to fully comprehend the scope of it. This is not a 9-5 job. Even if those happen to be your hours, you will find yourself carrying people's stories and struggles and tragedies with you long after you clock out for the day. I have found that there is such a delicate balance between setting boundaries with clients and becoming numb to them, and that cultivating this balance takes time.

I basically did not go through a job search at all. I got my job through a friend I met at my first-year field placement. I knew he was working for a drug and alcohol rehab and contacted him after I graduated in the summer to see if they were hiring. They happened to be hiring counselors, and he recommended me for the position. I went for an interview in July and was hired on the spot. I started working in September and remember feeling extremely fortunate, as many of my friends and former classmates did not find a job for months after they graduated, which is what I was expecting to happen in my case, as well.

I do not yet feel totally competent at what I do. However, I believe this is in large part due to the fact that my personal philosophy about working with people who suffer from drug addiction does not fit with my current agency's philosophy about how to work with these individuals. Because my personal philosophy is at odds with theirs, it has been a struggle to stand by my decisions, even if I genuinely feel that they are clinically sound. However, I do attribute my own lack of confidence mainly to the fact that I have been working within an agency culture that does not fit with my values. I truly believe that I will be able to feel more competent and confident in an agency that is more in line with my personal and professional values and expectations.

I could not have imagined how much I would learn in my first year as a drug and alcohol counselor. Aside from all of the imperfections and flaws of my agency, I cannot imagine a better training ground, specifically because it took me out of my comfort zone and pushed me to my limits, both clinically and emotionally (not to say that the two are mutually exclusive). A co-worker of mine joked that I have been through boot camp and now I'm ready for the army, and I actually felt that it was a fitting analogy.

Julia's story speaks to what Jenn, Victoria, and Mia have all said. First, the job search never looks the same for any two candidates. Second, it is very hard to find an agency culture that mirrors our internal values. This does not make the learning opportunities impossible—just much harder to detect. Sometimes what we learn from a job is that we have to leave, like Mia. Sometimes what we learn from the theoretical orientation of an agency is that ours is quite different, and our value base ends up forming in a reactionary way, which is still something and quite meaningful and significant. Further, everyone who wrote agreed on the fact that the bulk of their educational experiences took place in the first year out of school, rather than during school. It also appears that many of the issues that feel so stressful in school become secondary once you are finally in the field. And the issue of self care and self-preservation becomes one that is front and center and highly significant.

Self Care

The issue of achieving "good" self care at any time during one's social work career is a near universal one. First, what "good" self care means varies from social worker to social worker. Some social workers need to have exercise in place to clear their heads. Others need excellent group supervision. Let me try to discuss, though, why self care itself feels like such a complicated issue. Let me also attempt to address part of why there is something about the dialogue about self care that can feel so frustrating and odd.

Simply put, the work we do is exceptionally hard. Yes, there are a lot of professions that do very complicated and difficult work. I am not arguing that. I am arguing that social work is uniquely complex for the psyche to metabolize. The fact is that when we are performing our job well, we will see our clients walk out feeling tremendous relief. It is hard to say exactly why this relief is happening. There are a million reasons, and the reason is likely different every time. But there is likely a unifying reason why this relief is taking place, and that is because something transactional has occurred in the dyad between the client and the clinician.

Our Clients Are With Us

We ask our clients to rest their minds at our doorsteps. Many times, what we are also asking our clients to do is to part with significant pieces of their stress, to make them freer to function. But this stress, on a psychic level, has to go somewhere. I would argue that it floats into our minds, and it rents out space in the crevices and vacancies of our buildings. I think that as a social worker, it is fair to think of yourself as a building manager, with many different units, large and small. Clients come in and they make deposits in our minds—in our buildings—and we accept this. The clients don't stay forever, and we never know exactly how long they will stay, but we do hold things for them.

This is why, sometimes, we are in the shower and it feels as if we have a sudden realization about a client. We might be doing the dishes and the same thing will happen. We have our clients with us in ways that can feel both intimate and haunting. We have clients with us in ways that we can often feel ashamed about. This is because there is a lot of dialogue out there about boundaries and the need to have them. We need to have really good ones. That is true. But this dialogue often produces an internal sense of shame or a punitive feeling driven by an overly regulated super ego that keeps us from sharing just how truly "with" us our clients are.

I want to echo that Carl Jung spoke eloquently about a collective unconscious and a psychological field that we coexist in with our clients. This field does not end when our work day ends. Julia spoke to this very clearly in her narrative of her first year in the field. This fact does not dismantle, whether or not boundaries are present. But somehow, there is some confusion about all of this, and many new social workers are made to feel that if they take their work home with them, they have failed at creating good boundaries.

My hope is that self care begins with separating these two dialogues. There is an important dialogue to be had about boundaries. There is another important dialogue to be had about how intense our treatment relationships feel and that we often wake and sleep with this, which does not render us unprofessional, naïve, or ill-prepared for this work. Self care, in my opinion, begins with a level of acceptance about how deeply penetrating this work can feel, coupled with a surrendering of shame around that reality. We often conceive of self care as a highly behavioral intervention, and it can be. It is also a mindset that allows us to recognize the gravity of our work, the extent to which it is not fully understood by other fields, and the very dangerous way that we, as social workers, can inappropriately police each other's boundaries in a way that silences our very real experiences of having our clients as tenants.

Economics of Self Care

On a behavioral level, discussions about self care can be very socioeconomically strained. I had a few students in a class tell me that they felt particularly alienated by a fellow teacher who said that her self care took the form of a 3-week vacation to Maine every summer. I can understand the alienation. So much self care costs money and feels unattainable to social workers who are barely making ends meet. This is why Jenn's story about making use of her commute makes so much sense.

Any self care move that requires social workers to extend themselves beyond their resources becomes a source of shame, thereby taking it out of the category of self care. Yoga is expensive, and so is the gym. Supervision can be expensive, and so can conferences and subscriptions to academic journals that might be highly enriching. Embedded in the conversation about self care is a complex and invisible conversation about class that, to me, is an enactment around how we do not see social workers as part of a community of people who struggle socioeconomically. This perpetuates the us versus them dichotomy, social workers versus clients.

Peer Support for Self Care

My best advice, when it comes to self care, if I have any advice at all, is that you need to hang out with other social workers. This does not need to happen all the time, but I do think it needs to happen. I think it can and should happen inexpensively. I think it is important to find a community of peers with whom you can talk about all of this shamelessly, honestly, and where the complexity of your role is celebrated and recognized.

I do not believe that this is something that can easily happen with co-workers. Relationships among co-workers in agencies and nonprofit settings are notoriously complicated. Yes, there is certainly support to be had, and it happens all the time. The cultivation of relationships outside of the agency setting can be a sincerely saving grace, free of the daily politics that dominate your workplace. It will allow you to have a place where you get to say what you need to say freely.

Beyond hanging out with other social workers, it is of particular import, in our field, to do things that give you renewal. This sounds trite, because it has been said a million times. It can mean journaling, art, exercise. The bottom line, though, is that if you can't do those things for whatever reason, you need to pay close attention to protecting yourself from the shame that might ensue as a result. There is a very strong relationship between self care and shame, and this is something that I hope you can find yourselves feeling particularly on guard against. No one has the self care "thing" down. It is an elusive entity at best, so have patience for its unfolding and mysterious role in your life.

When To Say When

In Mia's reflection, she spoke about needing to leave her job. She is bringing up a very thorny issue about knowing when to say when. I would like to disabuse anyone reading this book of the notion that you need to stay at a job for a year. Yes, there is something to that idea traditionally. It does look good on a résumé. If you are crying yourself to sleep at night, it simply isn't worth it. I have supervised approximately 30 new graduates at this point, and I think that I can speak fairly clearly to when to "say when" versus when to stick it out for the résumé.

1. If you are not learning anything at all after four months and several conversations with your supervisor/boss, it is fair to consider leaving. I had a supervisee who spent her days in front of her computer surfing the Internet. There is almost no state of affairs that can be more demoralizing than this, after spending two years in school preparing to work with people. Fortunately, this is not an acute situation. In many ways, it is a powerful position to be in. She can easily stay at her job and keep collecting a paycheck while applying for other jobs. There is a sense of momentum when you are in school, and it is important not to lose too much of that when you are in the field. You will certainly lose some of it. That is just how it goes. At the same time, you are preparing for licensing and for a lifetime in the field, and you want to be very cautious to guard against stagnation.

Central to job satisfaction is stimulation, and after investing a substantial amount of time and money in your degree, it is okay to want this, to seek this, and expect this. It is also worth noting just how psychologically taxing, if not depressing, understimulation can feel. This is certainly something to take quite seriously without feeling as if you are "complaining" too much. It is a difficult trap to feel that you shouldn't be unhappy when you aren't actually working that hard. Work that is uninteresting, unchallenging, and understimulating can have a devastating psychological impact on you. Understimulating work is one of the most difficult and painful forms of work, and it is legitimate to take that fact very seriously.

2. Receiving no supervision for extremely difficult case material is a reason to consider leaving a job. I would never suggest that someone leave a job solely because of extremely difficult case material, unless for some reason, that material is particularly triggering as related to an unresolved past trauma of your own. By nature, clinical social work asks us to deal with extremely difficult case material. To properly manage this material clinically, you need to be properly supervised. This can mean a lot of different things. It can mean weekly, structured supervision. It can mean supervision that is out-of-agency and paid for by the agency or by you (if you feel you can afford it). It can mean you have found peers in your agency who are supportive.

The central issue that Mia was describing was a failure in the structure of her system, coupled with an onslaught of highly difficult case material, basically leaving her enslaved to work in a way that was highly unmetabolized. This is an issue that can and should be discussed in supervision. It is an issue to which you should expect a response. You can judge, comfortably, how out of control the situation is by studying your own symptomatology. Although I have argued that we all take our work "home" with us, or internalize it to some extent, we should not be drowning in affect around it to the point at which our daily functioning feels debilitated. Although it is completely innate to consider Maslow's hierarchy of human needs when thinking about our clients, we must also think about it when assessing the viability of our own employment. I am inserting a picture of it here. Take this with you when trying to understand whether your employment is sustainable for you right now.

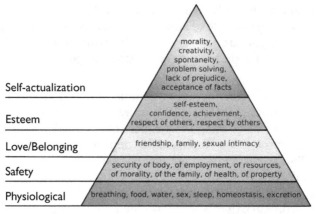

Image credit: J. Finkelstein

You will note in this picture just how many aspects of this hierarchy were missing for Mia when she decided to leave her job. Please gently consider this when assessing the sustainably of your own situations.

3. Ethical dilemmas. Both Julia and Victoria described ethical dilemmas in their agencies. It is not unusual to practice in a setting that challenges your value system. This is increasingly true in managed care environments. I would argue, surprisingly, that ethical dilemmas are not a reason to run from a job. Walk, maybe.

Julia was in a substance use disorders setting that was largely organized around very hierarchical principles—the staff is right; the client is wrong. The less clean time the client has, the less the client knows. The staff with substantial clean time is expert staff. Victoria's setting was largely organized around complex billing structures that began to erase the central needs of the individual aging client.

The fact is that this is our work. Social work lives and breathes in ethical minefields, and some are more complex than others. For a new social worker, this can be particularly tricky terrain to navigate, if not impossible. It depends on how strong the agency culture is. Other times, advocating for your clients in these exact settings is precisely the type of social work that needs to happen. It is activism, and it is powerful. It is hard to see ourselves as having to be subversive in our own settings, but I do believe that this is part of the responsibility of the social worker.

It is an intricate decision to make on your part as a new social worker: Can you stay and make change, or do you need to leave to learn how? These are both good questions, respectable questions, and the answer has to be a highly developmentally attuned one that is in accordance with what you feel you can handle at this stage of your career. You also have to be extremely on guard against becoming easily scapegoated as a new social worker in your agency who might be going against the grain. The point is that you don't want to lose yourself. Your first few jobs are largely about finding yourself, and this is never an easy process.

Assessing the ethical match between you and your employer ought to be a carefully calibrated study. Your conclusions don't necessarily add up to: "I leave" or "I don't." The one guiding point that I might lend is that it is very difficult to stay in a location where you feel an ethical mismatch without a single ally, and this often is a helpful choice point when trying to figure out if something is just too ethically uncomfortable.

4. There are a lot of reasons to leave when it comes to a social work job, not all of which need to be spelled out here. You might be ready for a new treatment population, a new modality, more direct service hours, a faster pace, a slower pace. But perhaps above all else, and I went more in-depth into this in Chapter 10, it is very difficult to stay at a job where you are not making a living wage. There is a tremendous amount of martyrdom in the field of social work. There are also outrageously low salaries. Be careful before taking or staying at a job where you can't continue to live your life. It will, very simply, make it nearly impossible to do good work. The amount of your paycheck and the strength of the work you can perform are not unrelated. If after an extremely taxing day of oncology social work, you can't afford groceries, your patients the next day will know it. Please forgive yourself for this fact, and try to find a salary that suits your life and your needs, so that you can fight for your clients and their needs.

Satisfaction

Although there are many reasons to leave a social work position, I can confidently say that for the most part, social workers love their jobs. In the chart below, you will see a breakdown of the responses of the 100 social workers I surveyed on their level of satisfaction in the field. This is a tremendously versatile degree that offers satisfaction in truly innumerable ways.

I had a student who was voicing an experience he had in placement. He is placed in a therapeutic school, a setting that is designed to meet the learning needs of students who are struggling with high emotional disregulation.

The client was a sixth grader struggling with long standing feelings of fear and rejection. She had a fleeting memory of a note she wrote to a boy she liked in first grade. She remembered how he had laughed and seeing him show the note to his friends, who also laughed. She cringed at the memory, but she left the session lighter—even happy. My student said, "So what do I do with that? What happens next? How will I know if this impacted any real change in the next session?" I realized during this exchange, during class, that so many substantial questions about our work were being asked.

Satisfaction in our work is highly intangible, and it comes in highly fleeting moments. There are many ways in which we want to solidify these moments, hold on to them, and have proof of them. I think that is so much of what the current advent of charting is about—the significant need for intense levels of "measurable goals" and documentation; this is all ultimately an intolerance of the ambiguity of our successes. To truly feel satisfaction in our work, a high tolerance for baby steps and the huge significance of these baby steps has to be enjoyed and recognized. Change–real change–is inherently incremental. We often don't even know it is happening. The student in sixth grade left the session feeling lighter, and that's huge. The deeper an appreciation we have for the subtlety and nuance of our accomplishments, the deeper the level of satisfaction we can experience.

Further, although this has likely been said in ways both trite and textured, change for our clients is inherently non-linear. It is so easy, when we are getting started in the field, to feel that we are somehow not doing our work when our clients regress or don't make clear progress. Satisfaction, client change, and client progress are easily and dangerously correlated. Know that client regression, if that is a fair and accurate term, is often a sign of large changes that clients are about to make and a sign of excellent work being done. The less you judge yourself on a day-to-day basis, the more likely you are to feel satisfied in the long term. This is a model for your clients, too. Satisfaction, in the field of social work, comes with significant patience, attention to subtlety, and respect for the nonlinear nature of evolution.

Self Disclosure and Use of Self

Many new clinicians appear to be terrified of self disclosure. I am not exactly sure where this terror comes from, but it has become clear to me that it has somehow become communicated that to let your clients know anything about you is "bad." I have done a lot of digging to try to interrogate the etiology of this concept, tracing some roots to Freud, of course, and some roots to unprocessed or incomplete conversations about countertransference in school. I would say that this has evolved, in my experience, into something that is akin to a near phobia in social workers. I would not argue for or against self disclosure–that is a highly debatable issue that could take the rest of this book to discuss. The problem is that newer clinicians seem to be withholding their instincts about how to best use their selves, because they are so frightened about inappropriately self disclosing or somehow becoming un-boundaried.

Yes, the conversation about boundaries is a very serious one. But I might hypothesize that the conversation has become some-what hyperbolic and overcorrected. Perhaps we need to think about how to use ourselves, a central tenet of our work, before fig-uring out how not to. Something about this dialogue feels inherently flipped to me, and I say that to try to give you some space to breathe around this dialogue that feels inherently, and perhaps unnecessar-ily, infused with fear.

Use of self and self disclosure are two completely different things. There are times—often, in fact—when self disclosure occurs in the service of use of self. That does not make the use of self any less paramount for the treatment.

In 1996, Raines stated that "One of the differences between so-cial work and the other therapeutic professions is the degree to which we meet people who have suffered malignant deprivations and losses...only the provision of an authentic person will suffice" (p. 373). Raines goes on to challenge us to move from being techni-cians (developing skills) and clinicians (using those skills, coupled with practice wisdom) to becoming magicians (using skills, practice wisdom, and self). What distinguishes a clinician from a magician is the use of self.

What these expert social work practitioners are saying is that this work is nothing without you—without your personality. The technique–any technique–is totally secondary to this fact. The use of personality has been endorsed by many social workers as far more important than any theoretical orientation. It has even been argued that "the practitioner has only one tool and that tool is her-self" (Elson, 1986, p. 3)–rendering the use of techniques as insepa-rable from a practitioner's style and behavior.

This leaves us with one central, unifying technique, and that is ultimately *authenticity*. The presence or fact of authenticity, which is characterized by a dialogue in a supportive and accepting environ-ment, can serve as a medium for self-exploration and change. Au-thenticity in a therapeutic relationship can assist a client in trans-forming perspective. It can be amazing to think that after all of the textbooks, manuals, trainings, and conferences, what we are ulti-mately left with is our own humanity to guide us–our own instincts, refined by training, education, and supervision.

You are going to want to be known, and that is okay

Embedded in the dialogue about use of self and self disclosure is the very real experience that you will want your clients to know you. There is nothing inherently right or wrong about this. It is just something worth acknowledging. The days in the field of social work can be long, and the relationships that we form with clients can start to feel painfully one-sided. There are many ways to deal with the reality. One includes strengthening your use of self, which can feel tremendously ameliorative. In other words, you may want to bring more of yourself into the work. Another way is to balance the work you are doing with other forms of relationships that feel more balanced and reciprocal. This can take the form of teaching, workshops, and writing. Simply put, though, it can become a toxic psychological space to be in to have a lot of information about a handful of clients and to go through your day never really feeling known.

There is not one way to deal with the wish to be known. Simply be aware that it is a healthy one and one that should be handled with tenderness and self respect rather than shame and self admonishment. There is a theme that I am referencing in this section–the very real possibility of falling into a pattern of feeling strong feelings of shame in this field. That is because, in my experience, I have seen my students, colleagues, and supervisees feel powerful moments of shame from sources that seem unnamed and unknown. I think that survival in the field of clinical social work requires a near vigilant stance against the onslaught of shaming forces that can leave us feeling inept and paralyzed.

Higher Licensure=Freedom

Wherever you live, there is a level of state social work licensure that comes two to three years after you have entered the field and have completed an adequate amount of clinical work and supervision. I can tell you that this higher level of licensure is completely liberating and life changing. It gives you a tremendous amount of authorship and flexibility over your career. It takes diligence to get there, but when you are there, your days and your work become your own. You can work privately, work in a different setting every day, work full time, or piece together many part-time gigs. It is up to you. The fact, though, is that at this time, the versatility of the degree, the education you have paid for, and the work you have done in the field begin to shed light on a future that can be extremely creative, lucrative, and exciting. There is no reason for your work in social work to ever feel staid, because the degree offers a good amount of flexibility. So go out there and diversify your days, your colleagues, and use yourself.

Some Voices of Veterans

Sometimes the clearest way to get a sense of the path forward is from others who have been there. Our field used to be organized around the principal of sharing "practice wisdom," which predates the current fixation on "evidence-based practices." In the following quotes, you will find some practice wisdom that might serve to guide you a bit on your journey.

Patty (clinical social worker with 44 years in psychoanalytically informed private practice)

I would hope that the social work profession would value, support, and help affirm training social workers with the extensive knowledge base available, so they can truly help individuals and families in their development and entitlement to good mental health. We can relieve depression and work with people over a life span, if necessary. We don't have to adhere to managed care or distorted corrupt policies. Many of us in the '60s and '70s had to leave agencies that were being run by mindless, uncaring boards that could not honor the needs of the people coming to them.

Susan

Beginner social workers should "get out there" and work—anywhere—as long as they are working in the field. If they want to specialize later on in doing therapy, that's fine—but first, a job in our field that gives them a chance to learn. Also, new social workers should be able to work with their supervisors, to like and respect them. I had a terrible experience with my first job, in a very prestigious psychoanalytic clinic in NYC. But my supervisor was haughty, arrogant, and dictatorial. All the students disliked her, including the medical students. I left after one year and found a job in an agency where I loved my supervisor and was able to learn under him. It was a good team.

Kim

The two things I would suggest are: (1) There is such a thing as "too much too soon." Learn when to slow down with a client and how not to overwhelm the process, and (2) When you are feeling stuck with a client, expand the system to treat more individuals within that system (e.g. couples/family work).

Marilyn

I think that those in the social work field should not be encouraged to launch out into individual practice unless they have had a good bit of their own personal therapy [and] have had further extensive training—both with study and individual supervision over several years. It is treacherous enough as a profession after many years' worth of experience, that great caution should be advised before entering the clinical field. Besides, dealing with insurance companies is not at all rewarding, and the amount they allow as payment is downright insulting!

Terri

I planned to work with juveniles in the court system when I got my undergrad degree, which is why I had a minor in corrections. I did my internship at a juvenile court, and they weren't hiring, but my supervisor recommended me to the local children's services agency. I got my first social work job there and liked it so much [that] I stayed in various positions for 25 years. Sometimes you just have an opportunity and go with it!

Chapter 13
What If I Love My Clients?

"It" happens to all of us. Feelings of intensity for one or even a few clients terrorize clinicians, new and old alike. Perhaps our fear of talking about it is born out of a tradition of knowing that parents are not "allowed" to have favorites. Or maybe it is indoctrinated into us by the fantasy that our work remains in the professional realm of our psyches, as if our psyches are perfectly compartmentalized. The fact is that doing this work well deeply accesses us, personally, and often leaves us reeling with feelings of rejection and joy, hate and love. We feel all sorts of things for our clients, both negative and positive. We do love our clients, and sometimes we hate our clients. That is okay. Sometimes this occurs because of complex transference and countertransference exchanges that occur between us. Sometimes a very solid and "real" relationship unfolds, and it can only be understood as such. And oftentimes, it is both; we have very real relationships with our clients that also reach deeply into our pasts and the pasts of our clients. In other words, many of our treatment relationships are simultaneously real and symbolic.

Underlying our ambivalence about discussing how much is at stake for us in feeling strongly toward our clients are conceptual struggles around the actual meaning of the treatment relationship and the role it is allowed to play in our psyches. It is hard to understand where and how this work should occupy our minds. It is hard to understand to what extent it is okay to feel stirred up or preoccupied. We are taught early on in our education to have "good boundaries." We know we shouldn't have sex with our clients. We even know that for the most part, we shouldn't give our clients a ride home (unless our job specifically calls for this). We are taught a lot about what not to do. This list of what not to do goes on and on. It often leaves us feeling afraid and more supervised by our superegos than anything else. We become inhibited about talking about strong feelings in supervision and with our colleagues.

In this book, I have covered, perhaps superficially, some of the ethical issues facing you in the field. There are issues of self care, boundary setting, and negotiating agency politics. The list goes on, of course. But sincerely, our ethics are most tested around our capacity to manage our strong feelings toward our clients. And this is also the place, when we are the most stirred up and moved, that our best work can happen.

I am also placing this chapter in this book because, as a newer therapist, I felt quite diminished and ashamed by feeling strongly for, or even loving, a client very early on in my work. By *love,* I am referring to affectional bond, a feeling of warmth, of positive countertransference. The word is intentionally broad, because it is experienced as such.

I had dreams about this client, felt very strong wishes for this client to become a part of my family, and would generally say that the contours of my mind felt deeply inhabited by pieces of her psyche. I simply did not feel as if this was something I could talk about in supervision. It was not something I learned about in school, and without my own therapy, I am not sure how I could have effectively managed this. I came to realize that love or deep caring and affection (on the part of the social worker) is a deconstruction of how we think of our professional, boundaried selves. In order not to fall apart completely in the face of it, we are required to attend to an unscathing level of honesty and self-awareness. This must occur in order for our more intense clinical experiences to be managed healthfully, rather than to the detriment of the client. For me, loving a client was at once exhilarating and terrifying. That is because love and social work are often both.

My hope in examining the reality of love or favoritism or deep affection in social work is to encourage us to not only permissively feel a range of complex emotional responses to our clients, but also to talk about it as much as we can, to give it sunlight and air to breathe. And, in some cases, we need to bring it into the actual treatment as a possible force for change and amelioration.

I have no certainty about how these feelings ought to be communicated, if at all. I do know that the sublimation of them can be toxic, that the celebration of them can be transformative, and that—most essentially—the acknowledgment of them must occur on a pervasive level in our field. I have never said "I love you" to a client, and I am not sure if I ever will. This does not change my strong conviction that silencing this phenomenon is complicated and malignant.

So, what if we just flat out love our clients? Many of us do. Are we cloaking this reality, the reality of how intensely we can feel toward our clients, that we can love our clients, in linguistic synonyms like "care," "empathy," "the therapeutic alliance," or "countertransference"? If so, this is a decision that, while potentially wise, must be carefully interrogated for its actual intent. Do we describe love instead of saying "love" to protect ourselves or our clients? And what about our clients who have never been told that they are loved? Is our withholding a reenactment or an obvious attendance to the professional frame? Perhaps it is both.

Having now taught hundreds of social work students, I cannot count the number of papers I have read from students who mention their countertransferential feelings and their plans to rid themselves of them. I wonder where those instructions came from. While in some echelons of our field, namely psychoanalytic communities, countertransference is increasingly welcomed, this does not appear to have trickled down. Similarly, while the "real relationship" characterized by an intersubjective nature is currently being embraced by some journals and institutes, the notion of having a "real" and potentially loving relationship with a client instills terror in young clinicians, who are increasingly taught to adhere to evidence-based and measurable techniques.

Ironically, it is precisely our less seasoned clinicians who deserve to be indoctrinated into the complex reality and nuanced experience that accompanies our work. We work, more times than not, in the murky realm of grayness that defies simple "right" or "wrong" answers. Manualized treatments seek to convince otherwise, but the tolerance for ambiguity that practicing social work requires, particularly when it is coupled with love and strong caring feelings, must also be a technique with which we equip members of our field.

I can recall a case presentation in a master's level class that I was teaching. A student was discussing a client who was chronically suicidal. She discussed feeling a sense of collegiality with the client, and during her presentation, when examining her fears about the client's mental well-being, she cried. Given the safe environment of the classroom, this was dealt with sensitively by the students, and there was a lot of mention of how "okay" it was to cry. It was, indeed, okay. However, when I met with the student outside of class, she reflected on this public and emotional outpouring and was unable to adequately trace the trajectory of her feelings. She remained mired in a profound struggle with shame while discussing the intensity of feelings she had for her client. I suggested the possibility that she was feeling a level of vulnerability consistently authored by presence of love. The profound and immediate relief that accompanied my naming of this possibility shifted the conversation in a way that only an utterance of truth can.

It is the utterance of the truth of love, of intensity, of vulnerability, and its pervasive presence in our work that I believe might make social work what it is–a holding environment for those who have been systemically disenfranchised that offers the possibility of an affectual experience that has not been available before. Social work is a field founded on the curative nature of the human relationship and the dismantling of hierarchical power structures, and we must examine the curative nature of every element of this relationship. We work with populations that are historically underserved, oppressed, and placed on the periphery of services that make living a sustainable life possible. What we neglect to say about these populations, though, is that they are frequently unloved. Many of our clients have gone most of their lives deprived of love, of being made to feel special. With this in mind, we must also recognize that social work is a field that seeks to end oppression, even in this form.

Understanding how to master our intense feelings toward clients, developing theory that informs technique on how to manage them, and realizing their curative potential is the work of social work.

If the relationship heals, what about it heals?

The underlying premise of social work, which is that "the relationship heals," needs to be revisited for its actual meaning. What is the relationship? What is it comprised of? Are love and relationships inextricably linked? And, if so, is there an inextricable link between social work and love? I believe that there is.

During any given day in the field of social work, I notice numerous exchanges occurring between me and my patients that are inspired by love. I hear the same from my supervisees. To the client who explains to me the sheer joy she feels at having just purchased an Apple computer, I say with complete sincerity, "Tell me more." I could take the story at face value and leave it at that, but I love her, and I want to know about the inner workings of this joy, about every facet of her decision to make this purchase. If I didn't feel this way about her, maybe I wouldn't care as much. But I truly do.

I hear a supervisee describe a 13-year-old rape victim and her attachment to this young girl. She doesn't know how to get her to start talking. She takes a desperate measure, putting her whole job on the line, and takes her pit bull to work. She knows her boss is terrified of pit bulls, and she is also aware of the reputation of the breed. She knows her client loves dogs. She chooses the client, thereby, in many ways choosing love. The client knows it and feels it. The client lies on the couch curled up with the dog, and she doesn't immediately tell her story, but things shift in the room. She starts looking forward to sessions, takes her shoes off, and gets cozier. She starts to experience a feeling of physical safety, exactly what was taken from her when she was raped.

The intervention isn't complex; it is loving and therefore transformative. This is not a love to which we are exposed in the theoretical discourse that informs our practice. I didn't learn about it in my master's degree or doctoral-level training. Really, no social workers have.

Where has the love been?

Plato introduced the notion of non-erotic or platonic love in the fourth or fifth century B.C.E. Plato asserted that love is an abiding, deep, spiritual connection that evolves between two individuals. He argued that this love exists without any form of sexual connection.

Given the seeming benignancy of this concept, it is surprising that a longstanding tradition of discouraging loving feelings within our work has held sway. The discouragement of platonic love has resulted in a paucity of research on the topic. This is not to say that such love has not existed between social workers and their clients; on the contrary, for as long as such love has existed, so too has the fear of acknowledging it professionally, whether in research or in supervision.

At a conference exploring the therapeutic relationship, one of our colleagues, Susan Baur (1997), powerfully observed the following:

> At a seminar on the feelings that clinicians have for their patients—a weeklong affair...I made marks in the left-hand margin of my notes every time the word "hate" was said and marks in the right-hand margin every time "love" was spoken. At the end of five days, [the ratio of hate to love was] forty to one.... When love for a client was mentioned—not love from a client, but a question such as "How did you handle your love for this woman?"—there was silence. (p. 221)

Baur goes on to hypothesize that the "illogical and deeply emotional forces that underlie the [therapeutic] relationship have seemed too close to romantic love to investigate safely" (p. 223). She explains that the exploration of these feelings is only sanctified if they are framed within the understanding of countertransference as paternal or maternal, but never structured in any other way that might be perceived as sexual and thereby threatening. Once a therapist mentions feelings other than those that mimic a parent-child relationship, she notes, little support is available from the clinical community. This feels very true to my experiences and to the experiences of many of my supervisees. You are allowed to feel only one way about your clients, and this one way falls under a very narrow and a superficially benign heading of corrective parenting.

Transference

One of the first ways that strong feelings and intense clinical feelings were understood was through the lens of transference, a clinical phenomenon articulated and crystallized by Sigmund Freud. Long before it was ever accepted to discuss our feelings toward our clients, Freud introduced the now very well worn idea of transference. It was Freud who first coined the definition of transference as he sought to make meaning from this therapeutic phenomenon. He was seeing a pattern of clients transferring historic expectations of past relationships onto the clinical relationship. He noticed that while some things felt like an organic evolution of the two people sitting together, there was something else happening that made treatment more complicated than that. He came to understand this transferring as a clinical opportunity for change. If a client came in and could transfer issues from the past into the present, the opportunity to work through and reshape one's experiences of history could occur. He saw transference as a largely unconscious process and understood the work of the clinician as a process that could aid in making the unconscious, conscious. Thereby, therapy would make the impact of one's own psychological history more transparent and understandable to the client.

In a social work textbook on clinical practice written by Joan Lesser and Marlene Cooper (2002), they write that the definition of transference is "a displacement of reactions originating with significant persons of early childhood" (p. 6). To Freud, the presence of transference made good treatment possible. He began to view transference as a source of data providing invaluable insight to the clinician. He also believed that transference, or the intense experience that the client has of the clinician, could serve as the arena for their therapeutic engagement. Transference became a pathway to deepen the therapeutic process and provided the clinician with a behind-the-scenes tour of a client's relational life.

Freud also sought to make particular sense of the importance of erotic transference or loving transference. He argued that the presence of erotic transference stems from the activation of past childhood conflicts and fantasies that are difficult to address sufficiently with words. He found that the stronger and more charged the transference was, the more productive and ripe the treatment could be. When he reflected on clients feeling love for their therapists, he argued that this meant the client was superimposing a wish for a strong comforter in the therapist, someone who could gratify and contain them at the same time. He felt that transferential love suggested the possibility of a therapist re-parenting and setting appropriate boundaries with a client in a way that lessens the overstimulation that they may have felt at the hands of inappropriate caregivers.

While Freud believed strongly in the curative power of transference, he pleaded for the erasure of countertransference. To him, countertransference was the eliciting of the clinician's past history by the client in ways that would lead the clinician to act inappropriately. He did not believe in the possibility for the exploration of mutual therapeutic experiences. It was not that Freud did not understand the complexity of countertransference—quite the opposite. Freud believed that our inner-child selves need to accept the frustration linked to a therapist's attempts to keep the patient at an arm's length.

> *The problem of countertransference is one of the most difficult in psychoanalytic technique. What is offered to the patient must never be spontaneous affect; rather it must always be expressed consciously. In some circumstances, a lot should be offered, but never anything arising directly from the analyst's unconscious. The analyst must always be aware of and overcome the countertransference to be free. However, at the same time, to give too little to a patient because the analyst loves him too much is to confuse him, and is a technical error. It is not easy and practice is required. (Freud, Jung letters, 1906-1913)*

Perhaps it is useful to note that Sigmund Freud was trained as a physician. Most likely, this background supported his antiseptic attitude toward the management of countertransference. Freud called for the analyst's role to mirror that of a surgeon—one characterized by detachment, complete emotional control, and sterility. Likening the analyst to a surgeon makes clear the message about countertransference. It is believed that the more emotionally involved a surgeon becomes, the more at risk the surgery is for failure. Freud believed the same was true of the relationship between an analyst's emotions and the analysis. What is most important to note about Freud as a surgeon is that, in many ways, we have a large amount of hand-me-downs from him. His thinking has fundamentally influenced us as a field. If the fit doesn't always feel right, it is because he wore a different size than we do. It fits, but only loosely.

How You Experience Transference

Now that I have described a highly intellectualized version of transference, I would like to attempt to make this more accessible for you. All of your clients are going to experience transference to you. There is nothing particularly good or bad or right or wrong about this; it just is. It might be helpful to access some of your own transference experiences. For every social work professor you had, you experienced a tremendous amount of transference. Let's say you read the professor's bio before class and see that the professor went to Harvard and has 25 publications. Chances are you walk in feeling a certain level of intimidation. Then, the professor doesn't even have the syllabus ready on the first day, and the transference shifts a bit. You realize that there is more to this story. Are these impressions? Yes, but layered on top of the impressions are your associations of these impressions. And layered upon these associations are your experiences of these associations.

I had a supervisee recently who felt extremely shaken by a very intense transference that a client had to her. He was a highly psychotic client who felt that she had repeatedly raped him. Her name was very similar to the name of his rapist, and her age was very similar to the age of his rapist when his assaults occurred. In her agency, the dominant modality was cognitive behavioral therapy, and she was repeatedly encouraged to reality test this with him, to help him to understand that she simply was not his rapist.

I don't know that transference can ever be reality tested. I think that it can certainly be used, and I do believe that its presence can almost always be beneficial. My feeling, in the transference example above—though extreme—is that the client is feeling safe enough to begin to explore some of the trauma that he experienced with his rapist in the context of a safe therapeutic environment. He does keep coming back, interestingly enough. The treatment certainly isn't mandated. Perhaps the coming back can be understood as a repetition compulsion. I also think it is an opportunity to have autonomy in a psychic realm that once felt chaotic and horrifying. Transference is past relationships making themselves known in the present. It is also past relationships trying to right themselves in the present. It is our work, as clinical social workers, to become vigilantly aware of these openings and to observe the best way to allow them to flow.

Some clients, because of transference, will become unconsciously dependent on us, and the experience of independence in our presence will be profoundly transformative. Others will become highly perfectionistic and invincible. Encouraging these clients to be seen in their imperfection and their vulnerability can be what shifts the way forward for them.

I recently had a student discuss running a group for rape survivors. She described a certain member who started to dress up more and more startlingly in group once she began co-facilitating it with a more senior clinician. It was easy to interpret this as somehow connected to something related to her sexual trauma, and on some level, it was probably connected. But the student, herself, presented as uniformly part of a very high level of socioeconomic society. Every outfit was perfect, every bag, and every shoe. When discussing what aspects of the student might be most triggering for the group, this nearly invisible fact to a class at an Ivy League university was completely debilitating to a group of women who were all struggling with extreme poverty, if not homelessness. The transference elicited by my student was one of complete socioeconomic shame. Had she not dressed this way, could this level of shame have been truly addressed in the group? Probably not. Was it the goal of the group? Definitely not. But the thing about transference is that it always untaps something, rarely intentionally, always importantly. Ultimately, the issue in the group, for reasons of sexual assault or identity, was shame. The transference got them there. But the student had to look at herself, painfully in fact, to allow the group to get there.

Countertransference

Freud first mentioned the term "countertransference" in 1910, and subsequently deemed it to be a dangerous and very threatening treatment obstacle. He basically argued that the more we authentically enter into clinical treatment, with most human and authentic selves, the more dangerous and impossible the treatment can become.

It was not until 1950 that the term reappeared in the writings of Donald Winnicott (*Hate in the Counter-Transference,* 1947/1994). Interestingly, while many of our hand-me-downs are from Freud, we also are left with the remnants of much of Winnicott, as well. If Freud plays the role of one of our intellectual parents, Winnicott is certainly a close uncle. And he paved the way, in addition to Ferenczi, for relational theorists, four decades later, to endorse the importance of an internal, private recognition of countertransference as important clinical data.

Although countertransference was slowly being deemed useful, limitations existed regarding the forms of countertransference that could and could not be discussed. Feelings of hate and disdain for clients were more readily acknowledged than loving, intense, or strongly positive longing feelings. Winnicott (1947/1994) shared a paper called "Hate in the Counter-Transference." This paper has been shared and taught over and over again. It quickly legitimized the powerful experience of hating clients, as well as the multiple ways in which this data could become useful in the clinical relationship. Winnicott examined the experience of hating psychotic patients. He wrote, "If we are to become able to be the analysts of psychotic patients, we must have reached down to very primitive things in ourselves" (Winnicott, from "Hate in the Counter-Transference," 1947/1994).

Winnicott went on to assert that a central primitive force is hate. This hate was normalized by his understanding of the mother-child relationship. "I suggest that the mother hates the baby before the baby hates the mother, and before the baby can know his mother hates him" (Winnicott, 1947/1994). Through this normalization of hateful feelings in the sacred mother-child dyad, Winnicott legitimized the recognition of a form of countertransference. He believed that the feelings between mother and child were most certainly mirrored within the therapeutic dyad. If a mother can hate her child, a therapist can most certainly hate his or her clients. While Winnicott certainly recognized that a large part of our work is to be "good enough," based on his writings on the idea of the good enough mother starting in 1953, he also served to legitimize a line of thinking about our clients as hateful. This legitimization occluded the more tender and desirous aspects of our treatment experiences, producing a feeling of shame around them.

Although there is a diverse literature exploring the experience of countertransferential hate, countertransferential love, longing, and affection are not given equal or even minimal recognition.

Sandor Ferenczi

It isn't that love, favoritism, or desire weren't trying to make their way into the canon. It is that the people who were talking about them weren't as popular as their contemporaries. Like so many dynamics on the school playground, the thinking that informs our field is a by-product of complex social interactions, some bullying, and a lot of tragic silencing of profound and radical thinkers.

Sandor Ferenczi, in fact, introduced the first mention of therapeutic love and mutuality in the 1920s. Ferenczi was a student of Freud's for 25 years. From 1908 (the day they met) through 1933 (when Ferenczi died), the two maintained an intense correspondence. This correspondence was an impassioned debate about the efficacy of different analytic stances, specifically the engaged versus the withholding stance. Freud called for sterility, self-discipline, and a therapeutic dyad defined by the clear hierarchy of analyst over analysand. Conversely, Ferenczi encouraged passion, equality, openness, and authenticity in clinical treatment. Nearly all that he espoused, with the exception of his call for highly blurred boundaries, echoes the hallmarks and values of clinical social work. This makes Ferenczi's absence from our shared social work curricula, and Freud's guaranteed presence, quite curious.

But the answer lies in Freud's power over Ferenczi on the analytic, intellectual playground. So, we were left with a certain narrative about who was even there and who wasn't. Freud tells the story and leaves an image of Ferenczi as a central and threatening character—one who challenged his ideals. But he was also one who might make us feel more clearly about how social work can be practiced clinically.

A potential hand-me-down from Ferenczi can be taken from an address he gave at The Hague in the early 20th century. In that speech, Ferenczi expressed his belief that "the progress of the cure bears no relation to the depth of the patient's theoretical insight, nor to the memories laid bare" (Stanton, 1991, p. 133). Instead, his method was based on a belief that clients were made well by sincerity, authenticity, full attunement, and love. Ferenczi believed that no clinical progress could be made if we maintain a distance through professional defensiveness with our clients. Whereas Freud considered distance to be a necessary therapeutic technique, Ferenczi called it a defense. Ferenczi encouraged the clinical surrendering of blind obedience, asserting that this obedience was what had oppressed patients as children; consequently, these very patients required tenderness. Ferenczi argued that patients sought something else—love. He felt that treatment outcomes were directly correlated with the amount of love given by the clinician to the client.

Despite Ferenczi's attempts to humanize the therapeutic relationship through the use of countertransference, Freud shunned him. Akin to the way social work is often shunned or relegated to the bottom of the clinical totem pole in many practice settings, Ferenczi's thinking faced a kind of censorship that has silenced an important part of work for nearly a century. Perhaps clinical social work lost one of its potential leaders, patriarchs, or mentors—a theorist who could have helped us truly organize our thinking around how complexly we often feel about our clients.

How will you experience countertransference?

Given this complex social and political reality, I want to clearly re-introduce the essential need for the honoring of countertransference, desire, and authenticity in your clinical work. If I were to tell you what countertransference is, I would say that it is everything. When you are with a client, it is how tired you feel, how awake you feel, how hungry you are. It is everything that you feel about yourself when you sit with your client, and it is everything you feel about your client. If you feel fat in your outfit, if you hate your boots, it is all of that. It is a fairly crazy-making phenomenon, because of the complexity of it all.

Part of what feels so befuddling about countertransference is that it is both real and unreal. So much of what we feel about our clients is informed by what is intrapsychic, in our own minds, predating our meeting with them. So much of what we feel about our clients is inserted into us by our clients, who are dislodging pieces of their own experiences and settling them in our minds. So much of what we feel about our clients is about the very tangible here-and-now experience that we have of them—the real relationship. It is all impossible and fruitless to distinguish, although it is sometimes useful to try.

Like transference, there is no right or wrong, rhyme or reason, to the presence of countertransference. It simply must be accepted and, ideally, used well. We have spent decades trained away from the use of it, even being told that perhaps we shouldn't work with clients who evoke "too much" of it. Maybe there are times when this is true. I would argue, though, that this line of thinking is quite dangerous and sets us up to not deal with very important parts of ourselves and of our clients. If we can't manage our work with our clients in a way that feels productive and progressive, of course, this is worthy of considering. However, if we are stirred up, I would not suggest that this is immediately an issue to move away from in treatment. Instead, I would wonder if there is a way in which this experience can be powerfully used as momentum or fuel in treatment.

The most accessible and simple way in which countertransference can be used is through the communication of affect. A student placed in a domestic violence shelter recently inquired about how she could best use her countertransference. She said that she frequently feels anxious, if not terrified, about her clients returning to their abusive partners. She said that at times like this, she finds that she becomes most intellectual and relies very heavily on psychoeducation to regulate her experience, offering pamphlets on cycles of violence and sharing information about support groups. Of course, these are highly useful interventions. But the timing and significance of the countertransference cannot be ignored. It is just too big of a possible clue.

Is the student responding to her own stuff? That is certainly a strong possibility, but a doubtful one, given the nature of the way our psyches deeply interact with each other in this field. She is probably aware of a wish, a pull, and a tug to return to an abuser at those moments. She is reading something in her clients that they might be aware of or not, or she could be wrong. In the worst case scenario, she is wrong, and they can tell her that. In the best-case scenario, she shares her countertransference in a way that opens up a vital dialogue. She could say to a client: "I am feeling anxious right now, and I am not sure what it is about. I am wondering if you could help me figure it out. Where are you in your process? How sure are you feeling about being able to commit to staying away from your abuser? Maybe these are my fears, or maybe these are yours. Can you help me figure this out?"

This is a classic way to make use of countertransference. It is acknowledgment of the co-creation of the shared clinical mind, and it is empowering the client to know what is what. It is opening a dialogue through the use of affect, and it is the complete deference of authority to the possibility that the client might know more than the clinician. This is how a social worker can and should use countertransference. We can run from our complex feelings, ensconce them within technique, or dig deeper through the careful and loving revelation of them.

Finding the Reality Between the Conscious and the Unconscious

Yes, there is a textured and long-standing history that has possibly led you to feel a complex set of emotions about how this work lives in you. However, this is only a very external and superficial explanation for how all this feels for you internally. The fact is that for each social worker's unique psyche, the intensity of this work is experienced distinctly. For some, there is intense shame, and for others there is intense pride. For most, there is both. To some extent, many of us dwell in feelings of secrecy around our work. There are whole hosts of "things" that we feel we are not entitled to feel or not allowed to feel. These are typically things that we feel that we are not entitled or allowed to feel in the rest of our lives. There are parallels to these processes.

I am saying all of this because I want to acknowledge the fact of it all. I am also saying it all because I think these realities exist somewhere between the conscious and unconscious realm for each of us. We know that we are open with ourselves about our work to a certain extent. We know that we are probably more self aware than almost any other practitioner in any other field. This is our dictum.

It is hard to say exactly what I am talking about, because the issue of this chapter is inherently elusive and abstract. What are we talking about? What is intensity? What is exactly unsayable? I had a supervisee say to me recently that she is terrified that it is only the clients that she "likes" that come back. She fears that the clients that she doesn't "like" know it and sense the rejection and don't return. It is exactly this level of fear that we all dwell within on some level. And it is essential to look at it, because I wonder if it is really clients that she likes and doesn't like. Do the categories shake out that neatly? Of course not. Nothing in our work is that simple. We are often so quick to either pathologize ourselves when a client doesn't return, because we think we did something wrong, or to blame the client. We settle for very dichotomous understandings of how things occur. The space that I am trying to encourage us to study, to stay in, is a very complex intersubjective, collective space that is created and very hard to be in.

Another supervisee of mine, who was a social worker in a school setting, continually observed her desperate wish to foster one of her students. Her use of supervision for this was perfect, powerful, and strengthened the work with her student. She came to understand what it was about this student that elicited these powerful responses in her. She also came to understand what she felt was missing in her own life that she wished this student could heal. Their work was powerful and painful. They grieved together in many ways for what could not be.

Perhaps unsurprisingly, during this intense process, the student was able to attach to a foster home for the first time after eight placements. The social worker also fell in love with a potential long-term partner. She could have fostered the student. That does happen. She saw it happen in her own school on many occasions and would ask me again and again why she couldn't do the same.

She could do the same. I thought it would be a missed opportunity for both of them—a missed opportunity to use the frame of our work. This frame allows our clients to reconnect with disavowed states of affect, moments of trauma and loss, in the context of a safe, predictable attachment that aims to work symbolically rather than literally. More possibility can be born out of our work if we study, carefully, what our desires are about and if we can allow for the clients to do the same. Rather than acting, we understand, we analyze, and we help our clients to do the same, setting the stage for their lives and for our own.

A Demonstration of Sorts

Below is a process recording between a new clinical social worker and her favorite patient. This is certainly the client who is occupying the most space in her mind—the client she is having the most time being honest about in supervision, and the client with whom she feels the most heavily identified. On Monday morning, when she wakes up, her session with this client is the part of her week that she most looks forward to. You likely can identify this part of the week for yourself.

You will notice that the most intense moments of love and affectual bonds are highlighted in bold.

Process Recording

Dialogue	*SW Process*	*CT Process*	*Analysis*
SW: So how is it that you can make it through the entire week without drinking, but then on the weekend, you binge?	I want to know what about the weekend triggers his binge drinking behaviors. Curious if he recognizes the link and is willing to acknowledge it.	CT appears exhausted, puffy around his eyes.	Trying to identify the precipitating event that leads to his weekly binge drinking episodes.

Dialogue	SW Process	CT Process	Analysis
CT: I guess cuz, you know, that's when everybody is supposed to be doing something...social.	I'm going to have to pull this out of him a bit.	Client seems frustrated with himself.	
SW: And you don't have anything to do?			Gathering information.
CT: Well, no... I mean, I have friends to call and I could call any one of them.	I notice he is smirking and smiling to avoid crying. He's not making as much eye contact as usual.	I don't think he wants to be by himself, but he is isolating himself because he feels depressed.	
SW: But you don't?			Still trying to figure out what leads to the binge drinking.
CT: No. I just want to be by myself.	He is on the verge of tears. I allow as much silence as I can tolerate before I speak again.	Client growing more sad and tearful.	
SW: You go into hiding and drink?			
CT: Yeah. Exactly. I don't want anyone to see me when I'm like that.		Client is trying to hold back tears, demonstrating difficulty talking.	
SW: You mentioned earlier that your mother doesn't like when you drink like that...she sounds concerned. Is she concerned?	**I feel like what I'm saying here is that I am concerned but I don't want to tell him that. Would that be use of self or self disclosure if I did?**		Highlighting CT's support network and how concerned they are, hoping that might enable CT to see what he is doing from a different perspective.

Dialogue	SW Process	CT Process	Analysis
CT: Yes, definitely. (Silence). I tell my family and my friends about Laura and they think it's no big deal... they say, oh don't worry about her, you'll find love...there will be more people in your life.	**God, he's killing me. He's in so much pain. It's thick in the room with his pain.** **My eyes feel hot and full of tears.**	Stops crying, becomes contemplative.	
SW: But it hurts... because it's more than just Laura.	**I am a bit reluctant to say this, but it feels right.**		Empathizing with how CT feels.
CT: What do you mean? Do you mean like I am projecting?		He is in agreement but might have expressed it differently than I did.	
SW: Projecting? Maybe...What I mean is that Laura represents all of your past relationship failures that are hurting you so much right now...I'm sure Laura is as wonderful as you say she is, but it wouldn't hurt so much if this was just about Laura.	Interesting how the word "projecting" is used so frequently in everyday conversation like a lot of other Freudian words.		Clarifying my interpretation. Use of self.
CT: Yeah...I agree with that...it's like I am projecting so much onto her.		Client is tearful.	
SW: Yes, okay, you can use that word... projecting.			
(Silence.)	**I feel incredibly sad.**		

Dialogue	SW Process	CT Process	Analysis
SW: Earlier you mentioned that you used to be an atheist, "full of hate," but that now, you aren't so full of hate. You said that you lightened up a bit. **But I can't help but notice as you are talking that I sense so much hatred toward yourself. What you are doing to yourself with the binge drinking...it's quite violent.**			More use of self, my own interpretations of what I am hearing. I am mirroring back what I hear. Clarifying.
CT: Yes.			
SW: You are your own worst enemy.			
CT: Yes... (Very tearful.) I hate to say this, but sometimes it feels so bad...I want to be out of control. Like, you see (CT shows me two scrapes on his arm), I don't even know where this came from.	Is he saying he hopes something bad will happen to him? Like death? Is he talking about death or is he talking about how good it feels to be out of his body when he's numbing out?	Tearful, demonstrating difficulty talking because he is trying to hold back tears. CT shows me two scrapes on his inner-left bicep.	
SW: Wow. You mean you don't remember?			
CT: Right.			
SW: Because you were so drunk?			

Dialogue	SW Process	CT Process	Analysis
CT: Right...it's almost like...(more tears) I want to be vulnerable when I'm like that. God, it feels awful to say this. SW: It's okay. CT: It's like, I want to be...	Feel uneasy, trying to listen very carefully.	Demonstrating difficulty talking because of trying to hold back tears, appears that he is horrified by his own thoughts. CT appears unsure how to articulate his dark feelings	Letting CT know that it's okay to cry. He doesn't have to hold it in.
SW: Do you want to be out of control? CT: Yes.	I need to gauge if he has any suicidal thoughts	He seems exasperated, like there is not enough time in our session to tell me everything he is feeling.	
SW: Do you hope maybe something might happen to you? CT: Well.. no, no, I don't want to get hurt.		CT very sad.	Clarifying his feelings as well as assessing for suicidal thoughts or feelings.
SW: But what you are doing is really hurtful. You are hurting yourself. CT: Yes. I am.			
SW: What's coming up for you right now? (Client was tearful.)			Helping him identify feelings that are making him cry.

Dialogue	SW Process	CT Process	Analysis
CT: I just feel like... why bother having all of these feelings if nothing is going to come of it? Like...I feel like I am preparing myself to die alone.	I'm a little confused, but I'm just trying to listen to his story. By "all these feelings" I think he is referring to loving feelings toward Laura. His biggest fear is that he will never be with anyone and die alone.		
SW: These feelings are going to take you somewhere good. I know it feels hard right now to be with yourself in this discomfort, but you have to do it so you can move forward. You can't numb it away. You have to feel these feelings in order to understand them. Do you want to stop drinking?			Offering encouragement and support for his decision to get sober.
CT: Yes, very much.			
SW: Okay. It's not going to be easy, but you can do it.		Looks a little improved in mood, but still very tired appearing.	

I wonder how you were feeling as you read that recording. Were you hoping she would say more about her experience of him? Were you hoping she would say less? I am particularly interested in how you felt when she said, "But I can't help but notice as you are talking that I sense so much hatred toward yourself. What you are doing to yourself with the binge drinking... it's quite violent." How did you feel as you were aware of her feeling: "I feel incredibly sad." In the exact moment that she was aware of how much she loved him—how attached to him she felt—she brought up her awareness of his own self-hatred. It is a fascinating intervention. It has a lot of sophistication. In a way, it is an interpretation of her countertransference as a reflection of an inversion of his projective identification. Or it is her own self-hatred for loving him, because she isn't supposed to be feeling this sad. Is it a vast move away from her very real affective experience? I wonder what it would have been like to stay closer to herself and closer to him in that moment. What would that have looked like? How would that have been social work?

This chapter is essentially about those choice points. What do we do in intense moments of intimacy? Do we move closer or further away? Do we move further from or closer to our clients, from ourselves, from our supervisors? And what does it look like to stay close? Her intervention certainly wasn't particularly distancing. It was lovely, in fact.

You are an attachment figure

No matter how you slice it, excellent clinical social work requires a certain use of yourself. Our clients will get attached to us, and we will get attached to them. If we are to truly honor the reality of attachment theory—which suggests that we are all driven by attachment, healed by attachment, and feel that the world is safer to explore from the secure base of a predictable attachment—then we know that our work is no exception.

We are attachment figures for our clients, and unsurprisingly, they are attachment figures for us. Relationships with our clients are deeply reciprocal ones that cannot exactly be lived as such, but are experienced as such nonetheless. Respecting the reality of the fact that these attachments are felt deeply will transform how we occupy our work, how we understand our work, and the breadth of what we will allow ourselves to feel in our work.

Part 5

Thinking Ahead

Chapter 14
What's Next?
Post-Graduate Options

For many who graduate with their MSWs, there is a paradoxical sense of exhaustion from the training and a strong feeling that the training has just begun. I have many students who, as they near graduation, ask me what they should do next. This question is partly informed by the inevitable feelings of incompetency that befall any new professional. It is a by-product of having a huge amount of knowledge that has not been completely synthesized and is not completely felt as real until it is practiced.

With all of that said, two years of training for the complexity of work that we do is somewhat short. The desire to continue training is largely based on the reality that much of our social work education feels highly generalized, and we hope to use our time post graduation to seek refinement. We are also often interested in seeking real specificity in our learning, technique, and specializations. This chapter will focus on post graduation options and how to decide on that huge question: What next?

I will start out by saying that the first answer to the question, "What next?" is: Wait. I cannot tell you a prescribed amount of time that any one person should wait, but I think it simply makes sense to wait some time before continuing your education in any formal way. First, many students graduate with the strong feeling that they know nothing. In my experience in working with supervisees, it takes about six months to realize what you do know.

Acting in response to the hasty anxiety of how things feel around graduation can land you spending money that you don't necessarily need to spend and making commitments to learning things that you already know. Let the knowledge sink in, and take some time to assess both the holes that feel most persistent in your learning and the places where your curiosity continues to feel most piqued as you start to enter the field and work with clients.

Another reason to wait is that there are many organizations that are well branded and well funded and are highly aware of your feelings of incompetency. The second that you graduate, you are going to start getting mailings and invitations to "continue your training." You are going to be on direct mailing lists and will become a prime target/customer. This goes, too, for classes that want to help prepare you for your licensing exams. You have just spent an inordinate amount of money on your education, and I think it is fair to want to wait a while to see how the field educates you before you start reinvesting further.

When the time comes, though, whenever that time is for you, there are ample opportunities to deepen your knowledge base, to broaden your peer group, and to immerse yourself more wholly into what is happening in the field.

Starting Small

Book Clubs

Some local clinical social work societies have book clubs that meet monthly or bi-monthly. This is a great way to get involved in dialogues after graduation. I suggest these as an entry point, because the shift from the student position to a collegial one takes some practice, and this is a great forum to try out some more assertive ways of being in your new role. It takes some time to move out of a hierarchical/competitive style of functioning into something more equality-based. Book clubs with colleagues of all different levels of experience are a valuable venue. Further, most of us (post graduation) are out of the habit of reading for something other than school. It is a wonderful thing to be able to move back into reading for intellectual pleasure, for our own desire, and for our own wish for deepening—not because it has been prescribed by a syllabus, but by our own motivation. Also, the best part of the book club is that they are completely free (except for the cost of the books, if not available through your local library).

Peer Supervision (Unled)

My favorite part of running my supervision groups is walking out and seeing the group continue on the sidewalk or in the lobby of my building. I think there is a real need for unled peer supervision. It allows new graduates to meet formally with each other to offer support, to problem solve about ways to manage issues that emerge as they enter the field, and to network with each other. Besides being free, it is a way to practice collegiality and networking, and it is a way to continue the relationships that you started in school.

Local Lectures/Seminars (One to Two Days)

Lectures at local hospitals and universities are an excellent way of getting your feet wet in terms of exposing yourself to highly specified and sophisticated dialogues on subjects that have always been of interest to you. It is important to be certain that these lectures offer continuing education units (CEUs). This is not because you need the credits yet, but because the presence of that level of certification is a sign that the lecture is somehow legitimatized in the field and worthy of investment. There are a variety of lectures all the time, all of which have entry fees. If you are lost as to which to attend, it is useful to consider the CEU piece as inclusion criteria.

Conferences

Large organizations such as the NASW, DIV 39 (the psychoanalytic arm of the American Psychological Association), the CSWE (Council on Social Work Education), the American Academy of Psychotherapists, SSWR (The Society for Social Work and Research), or AAPCSW (American Association for Psychoanalysis in Clinical Social Work) have nationwide or statewide conferences. These conferences are expensive and huge. That said, if one of these conferences happens to be in your location in one of the first two years after you graduate, I think it is definitely worth it to consider attending. First, there are almost always scholarships for new grads. Second, these conferences can be extremely energizing and inspiring. Presenters work extremely hard to get on the programs at these conferences, and for the most part, the information is cutting edge and highly relevant to our work in the moment. Further, the conferences almost feel like the opposite of school. You choose exactly what you want to do, navigate the landscape in whatever way feels most right to you, and are there for the sole purpose of enriching your own practice. Conferences also provide you with unmatched networking opportunities. They provide a unique opportunity to connect with experts in your area of interest from throughout the country and the world.

Bigger Commitments

Certificate programs

Many certificate programs are available to extend your training and to enhance your résumé. The range in depth, expense, length of training, and validity associated with the certification varies tremendously.

Certified Addiction Specialist

You don't have to be a social worker or even be licensed to be a certified addiction specialist. However, having your license as a social worker and your certification as an addiction specialist makes you highly employable when seeking work in drug and alcohol treatment settings. There is no question that this certification will set you apart from other applicants. There are three levels of certification–I, II, and Master, all of which require different levels of training depending on the state where you live. Training to become a certified addiction specialist can happen in a number of ways, both conventional and unconventional. For example, certain universities and training sites have highly reputable programs. The programs have about six courses each and are offered both in person and online. They require a good amount of supervision in a drug and alcohol setting. There are also programs through very highly esteemed treatment centers. Hazelden in Minnesota offers some of the best drug and alcohol treatment in the country, but it also offers some of the most rigorous training for professionals who are interested in specializing in this form of treatment. You can become a professional in residence or attend school there.

There are many, many ways to procure your career in addictions. If this is a route that you choose, your job prospects will likely always be secure. Your skills will long be considered invaluable. Your training will likely be based in a variety of twelve steps rhetoric, neurobiological aspects of addiction, CBT, and the various treatment modalities that are employed when working with addiction, which include both family and group treatment.

Psychotherapy Training Certificates

Nearly every theoretical orientation has an associated training certificate. This is true for each form of psychodynamic therapy: Object Relations, Self Psychology, and Ego Psychology. Certificates are available in different specialty areas, such as attachment based treatment for individuals and families. This is also certainly true for CBT, for which the opportunities for different forms of certification abound, both manualized and less formalized. Some programs last as long as two years, and some are six months. You can become certified in group therapy, family therapy, or couples therapy. These certifications are usually not affiliated with universities, but rather with training institutes that have long-standing and complex histories. That is not a comment that is supposed to have any negative connotation, but rather one that suggests institute histories are worthy of exploration before jumping in.

Trauma Certifications

There are several different types of trauma certification. For example, you can specialize in trauma while still in school by taking a few electives on the subject and securing the ability to list that on your résumé. There are also a vast number of trauma certificates available for you after you graduate. Because the field of trauma is expanding exponentially, it is impossible to list all of the possible ways to become certified in trauma. There are burgeoning areas of research on substance use disorders and trauma, working with veterans and trauma, and the role of sexual violence in trauma. There is also a growing focus on communities that struggled with long time exposure to violence in their neighborhoods, which might just be ravaged by poverty or might be actual war zones. The following is only the tip of the iceberg in terms of emerging opportunities to specialize in trauma treatment.

EMDR

Eye Movement Desensitization and Reprocessing (EMDR) therapy is a form of trauma treatment that is highly evidence-based, showing tremendous efficacy in more than 24 large clinical trials. Significant numbers of agencies are interested in clinicians who have exposure to this technique. The training takes place over two weekends. It is highly manualized and is designed to target very specific (usually single event) traumas.

It is believed that the use of EMDR can expedite a good amount of the healing that once was considered to take a long time to treat in traditional psychotherapy. The treatment is based on the premise that trauma perseveres because of blockages in the mind and that EMDR is a psychotherapy that enables people to heal from the symptoms through the removal of this blockage. Based on the belief that the mind is not very different from the body, EMDR seeks to unlock the natural healing pattern of the mind by restoring the mind to its balanced, pre-traumatic state to allow healing to unfold.

Although the treatment is not a heal-all by any stretch of the imagination, many agencies that work with complex trauma are interested in clinicians who are coming with a broad set of tools to begin to reset individuals on their path toward wellness. In terms of evidence-based, cutting edge treatments, it appears that EMDR has significant esteem. Given that the training is not extremely extensive, many have found it a useful adjunctive tool in their training and practice.

Military and Veteran Behavioral Health Post-Master's Certificate Program

Given the vast number of returning veterans from long and complex deployments, the need for specialized training to serve this population is certainly gaining in import and currency. Several universities are offering inter-disciplinary training opportunities for graduates of mental health programs. These certificates largely specialize in how to manage PTSD diagnosis and treatments. However, these programs also delve into other issues facing the military in an imminent manner. These issues include: studies of military culture and the deployment cycles, sleep issues related to deployments, traumatic brain injuries, substance use disorders in veterans, family struggles for veterans, prevention and assessment of suicidality in veterans, sexual assault in the military, and the latest research on cognitive processing therapies.

A good number of these trainings are offered through universities or university partnerships with VA centers. Some are through the VA alone or through the National Center for PTSD. The courses are frequently offered online and include a supervision component and some internship/placement experience. Because the research on returning vets is rapidly evolving and dynamic, these programs are one of the sole places where all of the most recent findings are being shared and taught. Again, this type of training will result in high employability.

Child Sexual Abuse Treatment Certificate Programs

Like many of the other certificate programs, a certificate in child sexual abuse treatment can be offered through universities or agencies that specialize in the treatment of this population. This training examines the complex developmental impact of childhood sexual abuse and the distinction between the processing of abuse in the child versus the adult mind. Trainees will learn the macro and micro causes of pervasive levels of childhood sexual abuse, will understand the role of play in the treatment of childhood sexual abuse, will likely be exposed to newly evolving narrative techniques, and will recognize how to make best use of social service agencies in the support of the treatment of sexual abuse. Many social work graduates leave school feeling particularly unprepared to work with children. Working with children who have been sexually abused feels much more complex and tender, and accentuating training with further exposure to literature, expertise, and exposure to this area can be highly transformative in terms of one's career trajectory.

These are just a handful of the available possibilities. The options are countless, which is a good and overwhelming fact. When considering a certificate option, here are some questions to keep in mind:

- Will my agency pay for it?
- Will I get a raise if I complete it?
- Will it clearly enhance my desirability for jobs that I am interested in? How do I know? Have I contacted potential employers to find out?
- Can I see the syllabus in advance?
- Is the faculty reputable?
- What is the class size?
- What is the affiliation of the certificate program? A university, agency, hospital? And what is the reputation of that affiliate?
- Can I speak to any certificate alums (and this is essential!)?

The Biggest Commitments

If on some level you feel that you are committed to extending your education in a decidedly long-term and significant way post graduation, there are three main ways to do this. The three ways are to get your DSW (Doctor of Social Work), your Ph.D. (Doctor of Philosophy in Social Work), or to continue to analytic training with an institute.

Most social workers who go on to get their doctorates have long known on some level that this was their plan. Fortunately, nearly all doctorate programs require two years in the field prior to admission. These two years are essential for both training purposes and to allow for a period of time to truly consider the depth of the commitment to further training in academia.

The DSW

As I write this, there are only a few DSW programs in the United States. This is somewhat interesting, given that the DSW degree used to have quite a bit of prominence and clout before becoming completely eclipsed by the Ph.D. The University of Pennsylvania re-introduced the DSW in the hopes of offering a clinical degree at the doctoral level for social workers who were hoping to become leaders in the field. With some exceptions, the DSW is inherently a clinical degree designed to expose students to the experts in the field on as many aspects of clinical social work as possible. Although the DSW program is interested in cultivating researchers, it is also interested in creating excellent writers and teachers in the field–two strengths that perhaps had been lacking in the service of powerful and increasing drives toward research dollars.

There are significant differences between DSW and Ph.D. degrees. Typically, the DSW does not take as long to complete. The DSW is typically unfunded by the university that is offering it, because the research that the students do is often not grant-funded or is not necessarily aligned with the interests of professors who are working on grants. This means that the DSW, although it may take less time to complete, is typically a very expensive endeavor requiring students to take out student loans.

The format for the writing of a dissertation for a DSW program is not as traditional as standard dissertations for many academic programs. Often, students can write two publishable articles, treatment manuals, or other forms of significant contributions to the field instead of the classic 5-chapter, original research driven dissertation that can take students several years to complete.

Further, the DSW takes place, for the most part, in the shape of the cohort model. This means that entering classes of DSW students typically graduate together. This is highly unlike the nature of Ph.D. programs, which typically have only two to five entering students a year who progress through the program at varying rates. The cohort model sets students up with a very strong group of peers/ colleagues that MSW programs cannot exactly offer, because of the different size of the programs. Students travel through the same classes together for three years. And because of the small size of DSW programs (class of 12-15), students typically graduate highly connected to one another, and their careers become somehow intertwined in meaningful ways for quite some time.

The issue with the DSW for many is that there isn't a clear reason to do it. That doesn't mean that there are not many reasons to do it, as there certainly are. With the Ph.D., though, the goal is fairly clear: a career in academia. For the DSW, the trajectory simply isn't as unfettered. Some do the DSW simply born out of an intellectual itch, a wish for more exposure to expertise, or to write and read more. Others do it in the hopes of advancement toward leadership positions in their agencies.

Many go for the DSW in the hopes of teaching, and many do teach. But a career in academia, as a DSW graduate, is not simple. The degree is not a traditional research degree, which means that DSW grads can be prepared for teaching positions at universities or colleges that focus on teaching (there are many), to teach as adjunct faculty (the opportunities are countless), or to serve in clinical/non-tenure track positions (which are available very rarely and are not necessarily offered with a renewable structure).

The DSW certainly opens doors, but because the degree is both new and old, the doors are not clear. It appears that—if anything—the DSW creates a certain level of entrepreneurial spirit in social workers, allowing them to become engaged in many different forms of social work leadership that include writing, consulting, teaching, supervision, and advanced practice.

All of that said, essentially, the DSW is an ideal degree for social workers with a thirst that feels both profound and generalized and who have a specific enough interest to create a dissertation. If there is a deep seated wish for publication and clinical refinement, and to have these skills honed within an academic institution and with the support of academic structure, the DSW is a highly viable option.

The Ph.D.

The Ph.D., quite distinct from the DSW, is anything but general. The Ph.D., instead, is designed for social workers who graduate with a very specific research interest. The Ph.D. provides the institutional support and funding to pursue research in a very focused manner. For the most part, one will not be accepted into a Ph.D. program without a clear vision for his or her research. This required level of intentionality means that students who pursue and become accepted into Ph.D. programs do so with extensive drive toward soundly articulated goals. As opposed to DSW students who seek a broadening of their MSW training, Ph.D. students are seeking a narrowing of an intriguing aspect of their training.

Many more schools offer Ph.D. programs in social work than DSW programs. Also, Ph.D. programs in social work are typically funded, meaning that students come into programs with the financial investment of a university backing them. Even if the training takes longer than a DSW (often 5-9 years), it is ultimately more affordable.

Whereas the DSW is largely strengthened by the peer relationships that are formed, the Ph.D. is strengthened by the mentorship relationships that are formed between advisors and students. Class work is secondary to research, and the dissertation is absolutely the central goal. Although achieving excellent writing is of huge import for the Ph.D., the production of original research trumps even that.

The Ph.D. provides a clear trajectory into academia, often offering graduates roles in teaching or research universities or colleges, depending on how many publications and grants were secured during one's time in school.

The Ph.D. is a very wise option for those who believe their impact will be best felt through policy change or the creation of original research. It is also ideal for those who feel that teaching on the undergraduate or graduate level is absolutely their calling or would like to consult with agencies providing direct practice on how to use evidence most productively.

Analytic Training

Analytic training offers the possibility of substantially immersing oneself in clinical training, outside of academia, in the service of solely practicing psychotherapy in a more intensive and long-term manner. Analytic training, if the training is done in a completely linear fashion, takes four years. What this means is that the trainee undergoes his or her own analysis, the coursework required by the institute, and supervision in tandem. This is a highly expensive and taxing endeavor on many levels–psychologically, in terms of the amount of time it consumes, and intellectually.

All of that said, by most accounts, analytic training is presumably a very enlivening process that enables social workers to submerge themselves into their work in a way that feels productive and consistently meaningful. There are many organizations that work to link psychoanalysis with social work values and encourage more social workers to practice in a psychoanalytically informed manner, arguing that underprivileged populations have been deprived of this type of treatment for too long.

Most urban areas have many analytic training institutes. More rural and suburban areas typically have a magnet location for analytic training that is positioned to serve wide geographical ranges.

How to Decide

Take your time, find mentors, and before making any choice, talk to as many alumnae of your choice as possible. To think of it in terms of an investment, make as objective a decision as you can based on sound and systematic research. How do people buy a car or a mutual fund? They go deep into the reviews, talk to the people they trust, examine past performance, and take the choice very seriously. This is your work, too, to become a savvy consumer of all the opportunities that are available to you in terms of how to proliferate the ways in which you inhabit your career.

And then there is your gut, which may know exactly what to do and always has. Yes, your gut–the anchor of the ship of any smoothly sailing social worker—may have the exact answer for you.

Chapter 15
Your Life's Work:
What Is Enough?

Getting your MSW entitles you to the possibility of a highly self-authored career. You can work from 9-5 or you can entirely create your own schedule on your own time. You can write, teach, work in a vast array of different settings, earn a lot of money, or earn a little bit of money. There is a profound amount of freedom in the securing of this degree. Although that is not immediately obvious or attainable right out of school, it is the truth of how your career can unfold. This level of authorship must be carefully and strategically sought, but it can certainly be achieved. Remarkably, this level of authorship is often coupled with the potential to do fulfilling and life sustaining work. I know there are other degrees; I just can't imagine why anyone would want to be anything other than a social worker.

This book is a guide. It is also a love letter to you as a social worker and to the field as a whole. The inequality and suffering we see on a daily basis is ours to fix, and we can do this while remaining fulfilled by the beauty, sensitivity, and flexibility of our work. Maybe I am an optimist, or maybe this field is really that enlivening and mighty.

So the question becomes: how can it become this enlivening and mighty for you? I have noticed, in my years of teaching social work students, that they frequently experience outrage, yet helplessness, regarding the social inequities and abuses they see. For example, there is awe when we discuss the impossibly small number of beds in homeless shelters in New York City for queer youth. There is discomfort and shock when we collectively realize that there are almost no resources available to children who have been sex trafficked and are living in Philadelphia. There is pain around the realization that as of 2015, there is no needle exchange program in the state of Indiana, despite the clear evidence documenting the efficacy of harm reduction.

I repeatedly tell students, when I witness their feelings of helplessness and pain, that this is the field where change can be created, and change ought to be born out of their responses. Graduates of

MSW programs are potential change agents. The fact of this reality, and the weight of this reality, come with the degree.

There Are Heroes Among Us

I thought it might be useful to share some stories of others who have felt helpless, but moved into action and created profound change, through the steady application of clinical social work principles. Perhaps you will hear echoes of your future story in these stories. I hope not, though. Because each of your own stories ought to be idiosyncratically your own, based on *your* passion, *your* capacity, and *your* outrage.

Rachel Lloyd

Rachel Lloyd is the founder and Chief Executive Officer of Girls Education and Mentoring Services (GEMS), in New York City. She started GEMS at her kitchen table with a borrowed computer and $30. She collected clothes from everyone she knew and let girls stay in her own apartment. Becoming a one-woman show, she did this because she refused to look away from stark trauma inflicted upon girls who had been sex trafficked or sexually exploited in some way. She recognized the systemic failure facing these girls. She knew that rather than being given support, these girls were often interfacing with the criminal justice system. She knew that educational, financial, and attachment opportunities were scarce, at best.

Lloyd now runs the largest agency in our country serving sexually exploited girls in need of support, mentorship, and positive attachment experiences. She has created a psychological paradigm shift, forcing us to see these "women" as children, these "criminals" as survivors. She knew that human trafficking generates $9.5 billion yearly in the United States. She also knew that approximately 300,000 children are at risk of being prostituted in the United States and that the average age of entry into prostitution for a child victim in the United States is 13-14 years old. And she refused to look away.

This refusal fueled Rachel to advocate for the passage of New York State's Safe Harbor for Sexually Exploited Children Act in 2008. This was the first law in the United States to protect trafficked young people. Since this advocacy and change in New York, 13 other states have followed suit.

But this is the macro level of her work. The micro level, the "clinical" level, is what is so powerful. It isn't that Rachel doesn't have boundaries or a professional versus personal self. It is that she proceeds into the work in a way that is unafraid and bold. She truly meets her clients where they are. She understands how attachment crises create resistance to support, and she fights past that resistance. She hugs her girls. She tells them that she loves them. Because she knows that change is almost universally nonlinear, she chases them when they run away. Because she knows that engagement is complex and often requires a team, she works with their families and enters their homes, if they have one. She tries to give the girls what they seem to need, based on what they communicate on a manifest and latent level, and she has saved many of them because of it.

There are so many of us who know about human trafficking, at least on a pre-conscious level. But to really let ourselves know about it, to feel the suffering of it, to feel the outrage of it–that is what can move you into your life's work. We can burn out, feel deadened, and feel hopeless when we disavow the pain of another. By moving into this pain–by looking at and acknowledging it–we find that there are ways to make true change. That is what makes social work so profound. It is the unflinching dedication to ameliorating the vast suffering created by inequity that makes Rachel different and can make all of us different from the rest.

The issue that Rachel ignored was the fear, the sheer inability to explain how she was going to do it. She certainly didn't have a business plan, and she didn't have start-up money. But the pain of not doing something seemed to outweigh the pain of doing something, and for that, many girls are better off than they ever would have been.

Carl Siciliano

Ali Forney was a gender non-conforming teen living in New York in the late 1990s. He left his home at the age of 13 and entered the foster care system, moving from home to home. Ali's instability in the foster care system was not and is not unusual for queer youth. In 1997, Ali was shot dead in Harlem, left to die on the street. At the time of Ali's death, Ali was actively engaged in advocacy for the homeless, LGBTQ population of New York City. A close friend, Carl Siciliano, took up the cause on Ali's behalf and launched the Ali Forney Center with only six beds in the basement of a church. The agency, at its inception, had no funding and no real support. It is now the largest agency dedicated to serving the homeless LGBTQ population in the United States. There are more than 10 sites, helping almost 1,500 youth per year with a continuum of services, ranging from drop-in counseling to housing.

Carl also employed a powerful, yet modest intervention. He assessed his populations based on their hierarchy of needs. He realized that without adequate housing, no real health is possible, particularly mental health. We are so often encouraged to create treatment plans, to help our clients articulate goals for wellness. But what if they have no place to sleep? Is it fair to have a treatment plan? I don't know the actual answer to these questions. But I do think that looking directly at the reality of our clients' lives alters our interventions. It gives us a higher chance of success, while creating the real possibility of allowing our clients to be truly seen.

Edward Eismann

In 1967, Edward Eismann became frustrated with service disengagement within a traditional agency setting. In his social worker role, he was expected to bring clients in for case management services and therapeutic support in a South Bronx, New York agency. He simply wasn't having any success. Rather than pathologize the clients, he decided to go and talk to them. He decided to literally meet them where they were. He started to meet with clients on their front stoops, in alleyways, and on street corners. He initiated a dialogue with them about what their community needed most. He recognized a deep and almost universal wish for family and for attachment.

Edward quickly became known as "Doc," and he created powerful bonds with informal community leaders. He then started leading therapy groups literally in the middle of the street, often stopping traffic in the process. Some of the groups started with five to seven people. They eventually grew to be as large as 175 members of the community. He created what was termed as a "tribal council," a "therapeutic community," and ultimately "symbolic families." These families lent unyielding support to each other, standing in for absent parents, addicted siblings, and imprisoned caregivers. Edward's communities are still going strong today. Ten years later, in 1977, it became an independent nonprofit agency called UNITAS. As of 2015, the agency is providing trainings to schools and other agencies on how to foster engagement and create informal, healing communities.

Edward is so much like Rachel and Carl. He refused to see the clients as the problem. He refused to pathologize the victims of poverty and suffering and, instead, sought to truly understand them. Agency culture is powerfully drawn, oftentimes, to neglecting clients who are persistent "no-shows." Sometimes we label these clients as having Borderline Personality Disorder; other times we just reduce our understanding of them as "resistant." Edward could have done this, too. It would have been a lot easier. However, sensing that the problem was not the clients themselves, but something deeper, Edward decided simply to ask his clients for answers and clarity. This choice is so powerfully elegant in its simplicity. Some of our best interventions are.

Rachel has been recognized by the UN, and Carl has been recognized by President Obama. Edward has one of the most long running and successful nonprofit agencies in our country's largest city. They all knew that the problem was the system, not the clients who were trying to survive the system. They all sought to clinically engage their treatment populations through ultimately bold interventions that started small, started humbly, and started by following the lead of the real experts in our field—our clients.

Erica

On a smaller, yet still essential note, there is Erica. Erica is also a change agent who is making organic baby blankets. Erica sells them and donates a large part of the proceeds to children in need of proper educational supplies. She believes that a large part of the rise in autism and ADHD among children is due to environmental toxins. When she thinks about it, it makes it hard for her to breathe. She imagines the CEOs of large companies looking at two options for how to make materials for children and choosing the cheaper options every time, increasing their own bottom line. She pictures their awareness of the slave labor that it will take to maintain the bottom line, and her blood boils, leaving her feeling panicked and deeply unsettled.

She reflects on it all the time: *Why am I so different? Why can't I just buy my kids clothes like everyone else does?* She wonders if she is crazy. I wonder, too, *is she crazy?* I don't think so. But in a society in which we are trained into dissociation, where we are habituated into walking past someone homeless and hungry on the street, I see why she feels left out. So, she sews. She sews soft, organic, toxin-free blankets. She never feels as if it is enough, but she feels it is what she can do. She feels it is where her talent lies. She does it to feel a little less insane. I think that maybe it will make the world saner.

I don't mean to share Rachel, Carl, Edward, or Erica's stories to set the goal post high. Instead, I am sharing them because seeing clearly, and embracing what is clearly seen, changes us and moves us forward, toward the direction of our life's work. When I hear about Rachel and Carl, it makes me feel small, but powerful. It reminds me that the change lies in our field, in our awareness, and in our own power. It also reminds me that change is slow. I imagine Rachel ran out of her $30 quickly and that Carl instantly realized that six beds are not very many. I imagine that Edward felt incredibly awkward hanging out on a street corner in his "dress" clothes. I imagine that Erica feels that sewing takes a ridiculously long time without the labor provided by a factory. I imagine that all of this started out feeling like a lot less than enough.

You Can't Do It All

But it never feels like enough. I get it. There is an overwhelming feeling in the field of social work that we are responsible for all of the change in the world. This often leaves us feeling overwhelmed and befuddled. There are days when I feel so pained by different social inequities that I don't know where to start, and I don't know where to stop. Sometimes I just think that it would be easier to take a nap.

One month before Bobby Kennedy died, he was asked about what he wanted his obituary to say. During that time, I imagine it was impossible to not have an answer to that question readily prepared. He said:

Something about the fact that I made some contribution to either my country, or those who were less well off. I think back to what Camus wrote about the fact that perhaps this world is a world in which children suffer, but we can lessen the number of suffering children, and if you do not do this, then who will do this? I'd like to feel that I'd done something to lessen that suffering. There are children in the Mississippi Delta whose bellies are swollen with hunger.... Many of them cannot go to school because they have no clothes or shoes. These conditions are not confined to rural Mississippi. They exist in dark tenements in Washington, D.C., within sight of the Capitol, in Harlem, in South Side Chicago, in Watts. There are children in each of these areas who have never been to school, never seen a doctor or a dentist. There are children who have never heard a conversation in their homes, never read or even seen a book. ("Biography," n.d.)

He responded to his own commentary and reflection by saying, "Each time a man stands up for an ideal, or acts to improve the lot of others, or strikes out against injustice, he sends forth a tiny ripple of hope, and crossing each other from a million different centers of energy and daring, those ripples build a current that can sweep down the mightiest walls of oppression and resistance." He continued, "We will not stand by or be aloof. We will move."

What is moving? We are moving when we strive to provide enough. Enough is the capacity to patiently bear witness, to listen, to suffer, to encourage, to support, to grieve with, to understand, to empathize, to struggle. This is so much more than what most people are receiving. It is enough because our intention, our authenticity, and our transparency are a gift to others—a gift that is not plentiful by any means. It is a rarity to truly show up, to make metaphoric eye contact, to think about how people are trying and trying hard.

Winnicott argues for the provision of the "good enough mother." I would argue that in many ways, we need to operate in this spirit. The good enough mother is attuned to the needs of her child, attends to subtle and overt communication cues, and provides opportunities for both intimacy and distance. This attunement makes the child feel seen and welcome. We mirror the intensity of emotional experiences like joy and distress. We offer both acknowledgment and containment. We do this to help our clients negotiate the world successfully and in a less isolated state.

With Winnicott's ideals in mind, I think about Bobby Kennedy's speech about desolation and poverty. He asks that we ameliorate the suffering of children. Our clients are sometimes children and are sometimes *inner* children.

I think about a supervisee of mine. She is working in a large charter school system. The school requires strict uniforms, black shoes, and black belts. One of her students cannot afford black shoes. His mom has told my supervisee many times that she just can't swing it. When he gets to school without his shoes, instead of sending him home, the administrators know to send him to her. She keeps shoes in her office, just his size. He borrows them for the day. It is against the "rules" to give them to him. No "gifts" can be exchanged. Yet he gets to go to school, gets the gift of her intention and love, and he gets the shoes for enough time.

Just enough.

References

Baur, S. (1997). *The intimate hour.* New York, NY: Houghton Mifflin.

Biography. (n.d.) In *Robert F. Kennedy.* JFK Lancer Publications & Productions. Retrieved from *http://bobby-kennedy.com/rfkbiography.htm.*

Center for Clinical Social Work. (2008). *A model practice act for clinical social work.* Salem, MA: Center for Clinical Social Work.

Elson, M. (1986). *Self psychology in clinical social work,* New York: W.W. Norton.

Frawley-O'Dea, M. G. & Sarnat, J. E. (2001). *The supervisory relationship.* New York: Guilford Press.

Freud, S., & Jung, C.G. (1994). *The Freud-Jung letters: The correspondence between Sigmund Freud and Carl Gustav Jung (1906–1913).* McGuire, W., ed. London: Routledge and the Hogarth Press.

Hudson, C. (2005). Socioeconomic status and mental illness: Tests of the social causation and selection hypotheses. *American Journal of Orthopsychiatry. 75* (1), 3-18.

Kennedy, S. (2002). *Prosperity pie: How to relax about money and everything else.* New York: Touchstone Press.

Lesser, J. G., & Cooper, M. (2002). *Clinical social work practice: An integrated approach.* New York: Pearson.

Mitchell, S. (1988). *Relational concepts in psychoanalysis.* Boston: Harvard University Press.

National Association of Social Workers. (2008). *Code of ethics of the National Association of Social Workers.* Washington, D.C.: NASW Press.

National Association of Social Workers. (2005). *NASW standards for clinical social work in social work practice.* Washington, D.C.: National Association of Social Workers.

Raines, J. (1996). Self-disclosure in clinical social work. *Clinical Social Work Journal, 24* (4), 357–375.

Rosenthal, M. (2015). *Your life after trauma: Powerful practices to reclaim your identity.* New York: W.W. Norton.

Stanton, M. (1991). *Sándor Ferenczi: Reconsidering active intervention.* Northvale, NJ: Aronson Press.

Stepansky, P. E., & Goldberg, A. (Eds.). (1984). *Kohut's legacy: Contributions to self psychology.* Hillsdale, NJ: The Analytic Press.

Weick, A., Rapp, C., Sullivan, W. P., & Kisthardt, W. (1989). A strengths perspective for social work practice. *Social Work, 34* (4), 350-354.

Winnicott, D. W. (1994). Hate in the counter-transference. *The Journal of Psychotherapy Practice and Research, 3* (4), 348–356.

Index

About the Author

Dr. Danna Bodenheimer, LCSW, lives and works in Philadelphia, PA. After leaving New York City in 2004, she had no idea that love for another city was possible. But working and living as a social worker in Philadelphia has demonstrated, for her, the beauty of her city.

Danna graduated from Smith College, earning her bachelor's degree in Women's Studies. After wholeheartedly planning on attending a Ph.D. program in psychology, going so far as to get her post-baccalaureate degree in psychology from Columbia University, Danna discovered the intricate beauty and possibility that social work offers. Turning down psychology programs to receive her MSW from Smith College, and returning to her educational roots in Northampton, Danna found her clinical self. After completing two internships in Philadelphia, one in a partial day treatment program and another at a school for psychoanalysis, Danna began her career at the Tuttleman Counseling Center at Temple University.

Three years later, while in the middle of her doctoral studies at the University of Pennsylvania, where she received her DSW, Danna began a teaching career and her own private practice. Having taught at Rutgers, Temple, and the University of Pennsylvania, Danna has settled into teaching at Bryn Mawr's Graduate School of Social Work and Social Research. She teaches clinical practice and classes on gender and sexuality. Danna is now the head of the Walnut Psychotherapy Center, a trauma-informed outpatient setting that she founded, specializing in the treatment of the LGBTQ population.

Danna spends her time supervising, practicing psychotherapy, teaching, and consulting. She is the mother of two amazing young boys and lives in Philadelphia with her wife. She uses Philadelphia as a landscape to study issues of oppression, intersecting identities, and complex socioeconomic struggle.

Danna received the 2011-2012 Award for Excellence in Teaching from the University of Pennsylvania. She was also selected as a fellow for the American Psychoanalytic Association for 2012-2013. She is a licensed clinical social worker (LCSW) in Pennsylvania.

Social Work Titles Published by White Hat Communications

Real World Clinical Social Work *(published by The New Social Worker Press, imprint of White Hat Communications)*
Days in the Lives of Social Workers
More Days in the Lives of Social Workers
Days in the Lives of Gerontological Social Workers
Riding the Mutual Aid Bus and Other Adventures in Group Work
Beginnings, Middles, & Ends
Is It Ethical?
The Field Placement Survival Guide
The Social Work Graduate School Applicant's Handbook
The New Social Worker Magazine

Visit us online at:

The New Social Worker Online
http://www.socialworker.com

SocialWorkJobBank
http://www.socialworkjobbank.com

White Hat Communications Store
http://shop.whitehatcommunications.com

Network with us:

http://www.facebook.com/newsocialworker
http://www.facebook.com/socialworkjobbank
http://www.facebook.com/daysinthelivesofsocialworkers
http://www.facebook.com/whitehatcommunications
http://www.twitter.com/newsocialworker
http://www.linkedin.com/groups?gid=3041069
https://plus.google.com/101612885418842828982/posts